Rhine River Cruise Travel Guide 2025

Top Destinations With Map & Images, Quaint Villages, Scenic Vineyards and Landscapes River Valley, Excursions And Activities at Every Stop. Bonus Inside

By

Darrin C. Erviny

Copyright © 2025 by Darrin C. Ervin. All rights reserved.

No part of this publication may be reproduced, distributed, or transmitted in any form or by any means, including photocopying, recording, or other electronic or mechanical methods, without the prior written permission of the author, except in the case of brief quotations used in book reviews and other non-commercial uses as permitted by copyright law.

This book is a work of nonfiction. While every effort has been made to ensure accuracy, the author and publisher assume no responsibility for errors, omissions, or changes in details after the time of publication. The information in this guide is for general purposes only and should not be used as a substitute for professional advice or official travel guidelines.

Trademark Disclaimer

All trademarks, service marks, product names, and company names or logos appearing in this book are the property of their respective owners. Their inclusion is solely for informational purposes and does not imply sponsorship, endorsement, or affiliation with this book or the author.

This book is an independent publication and is not authorized, sponsored, or endorsed by any entities, organizations, or companies mentioned herein. Any references to specific trademarks or brands are for descriptive purposes only and do not constitute or imply any claim of ownership or rights to those trademarks.

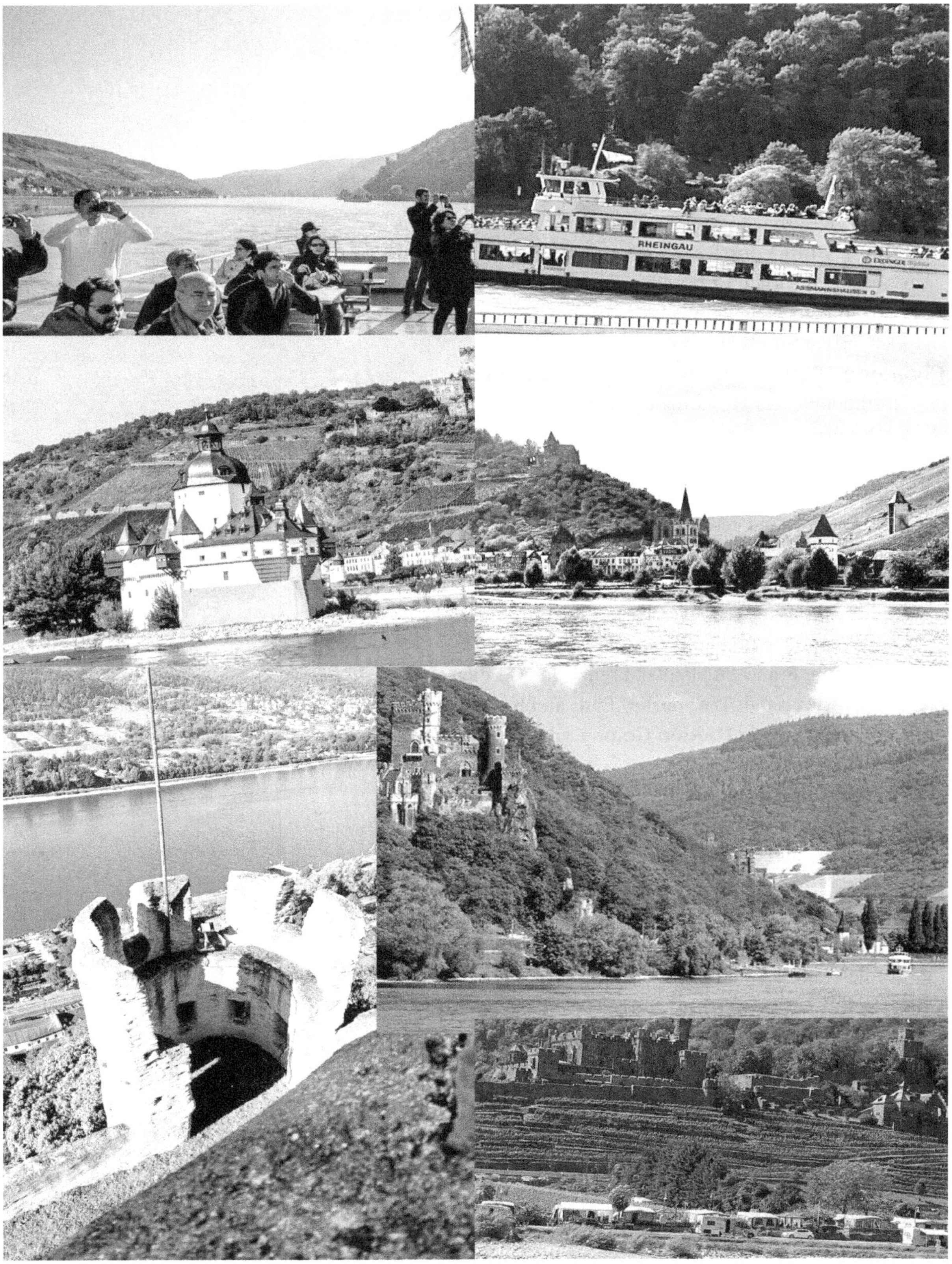
RHEINGAU

Table Of Content

Chapter 1. An Introduction to the Rhine River Cruise — 5
   Overview of the Rhine River. — 5
   It is the best time to cruise. — 8

Chapter 2. Plan Your Rhine River Journey — 10
   Choosing the Right Cruise Line — 10
   Budgeting for Your Trip — 11
   Packing Essentials for a River Cruise — 14

Chapter 3. Popular Rhine River Cruise Routes — 18
   Northbound versus Southbound Itineraries — 18
   Customise Your Cruise Experience — 20

Chapter 4. Top destinations and stopovers — 24
   Amsterdam, Netherlands: Gateway to the Rhine — 24
   How to Get to Amsterdam — 26
   Cologne, Germany: The Iconic Cathedral and Historic Sites — 28
   Koblenz: The meeting of the Rhine and Moselle rivers — 31
   Rüdesheim: Wine Country Charm. — 34
   Heidelberg: The Romantic City of Castles. — 36
   Strasbourg, France: A blend of French and German culture. — 38
   Basel, Switzerland: The Journey Ends and Beyond — 40

Chapter 5. Discover Hidden Gems and Quaint Villages — 45
   St. Goar and Lorelei Rock — 45
   Breisach: The Gateway to the Black Forest. — 46

Chapter 6. Onboard Activities and Entertainment — 48
   Local Wine and Cuisine Tastings — 48

Chapter 7. Must-See Landmarks along the Rhine — 51
   Rhine castles and mediaeval ruins — 51
   UNESCO World Heritage Sites — 53
   Scenic Vineyards and Landscapes River Valley — 56

Chapter 8. Excursions and Activities at Every Stop — 58
   Guided Walking Tours — 58
   Bike and Hike Along the Rhine — 59
   Riverfront Cafés and Local Markets — 60

Chapter 9. Practical Tips for a Smooth Cruise. — 62
   Understanding Local Culture and Etiquette. — 62
   Local Customs and Etiquette — 62
   Transportation — 63
   Currency and Payment Tips — 76
   Health, Safety, and Insurance — 77

Chapter 10 concludes with "Embrace the Magic of the Rhine." — 80

Make the Most of Your River Journey	80
Final thoughts and farewell.	81
Useful resources and contact information for arranging a vacation to the Rhine River:	82
Bonus Section(Expert Photography Tips & Travel Journal)	83

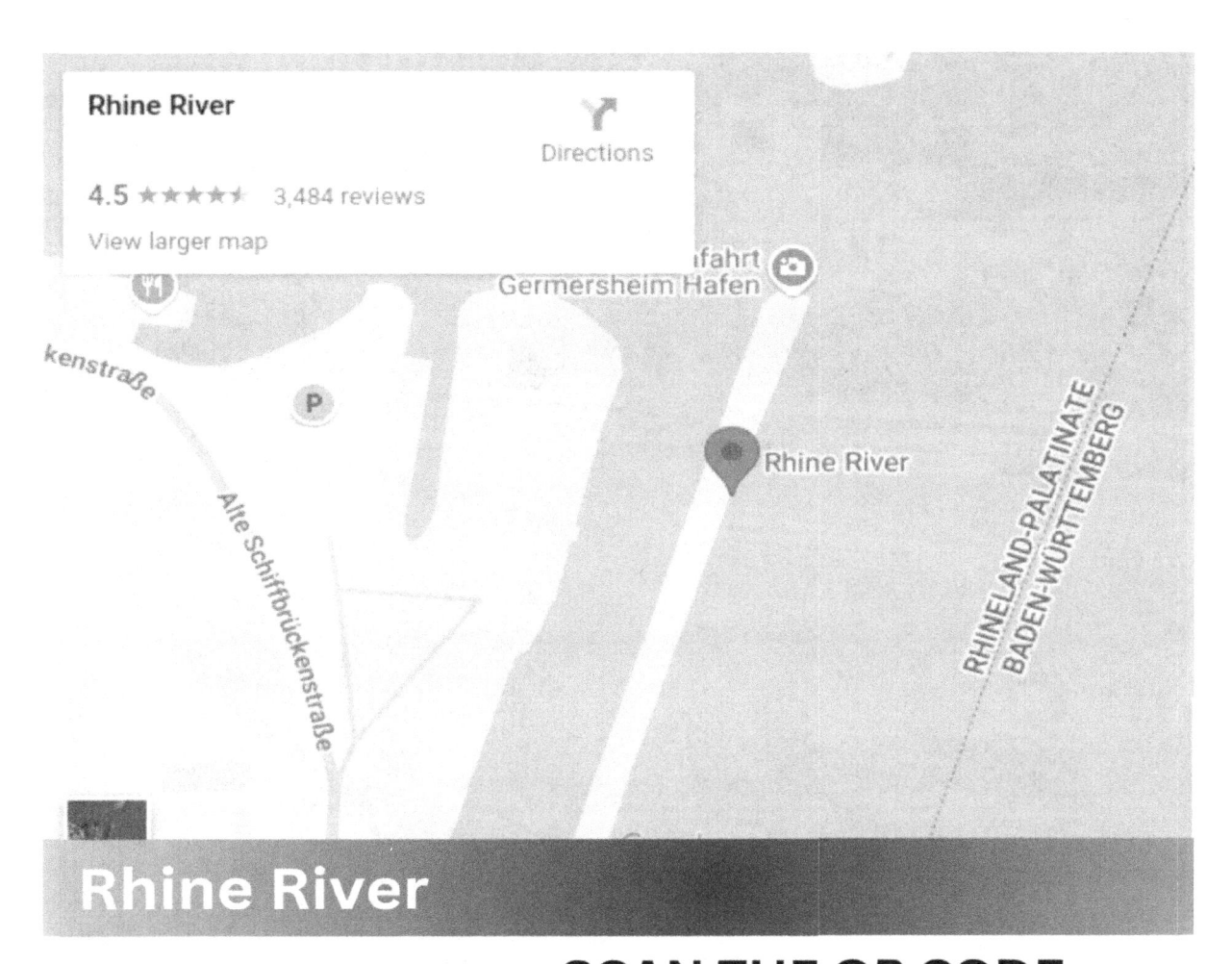

SCAN THE QR CODE

1. Open your device's camera app.
2. Align the QR code within the camera frame.
3. Wait for the code to be recognized.
4. Check the displayed notification or link.
5. Tap to access the linked content or information.

Chapter 1. An Introduction to the Rhine River Cruise

Overview of the Rhine River.

The Rhine River flows from the Swiss Alps through Germany, France, and the Netherlands before draining into the North Sea. As I floated down its tranquil waters, I couldn't help but feel a strong connection to the Rhine's centuries of history—its banks dotted with mediaeval castles, terraced vineyards, and tiny towns that seem undisturbed by time.

Throughout European history, the Rhine has been more than simply a river; it has served as an important lifeblood for commerce, culture, and communication. Navigating this river gives a unique chance to cruise through places that were previously crucial to the Roman Empire, medieval kingdoms, and major trading centres. The river's stunning beauty is only matched by its cultural depth.

The shifting vistas along the Rhine were mesmerising from the cruise ship's deck—rolling vineyards gave way to wooded hills and towering cliffs. The legendary Middle Rhine Valley, a UNESCO World Heritage Site, was especially magnificent. The castles placed on hilltops seemed like sentinels watching the river below, each with its history and traditions. It's difficult to imagine a more picturesque setting for travel, and I immediately understood why the Rhine River has inspired poets, painters, and musicians for ages.

For me, the Rhine River was more than simply the breathtaking vistas—it was about the sensation of stepping into the past, into a world where every curve in the river revealed a new chapter of history, a new treasure waiting to be discovered. Cruising the Rhine is more than a holiday; it's an adventure through time.

The History and Significance of Rhine River Cruises

For almost two millennia, the Rhine River has served as an important artery of commerce, travel, and culture across Europe. Its significance stretches back to the Roman Empire, when it functioned as a vital military and commercial route, defining the northern border of Roman holdings. Throughout the years, the river has played an important role in European politics, economy, and culture, passing through six nations and serving as a natural connector between different areas.

Rhine River cruises, however, are a comparatively contemporary phenomenon that originated in the late 19th and early 20th centuries. As industrialisation made Europe more accessible and travel more inexpensive, the Rhine's visual beauty and cultural riches started to draw visitors. Early cruises appealed to European aristocrats looking for a relaxing getaway from city life, fascinated by the river's scenic vistas, mediaeval castles, and quaint villages. The Rhine's romanticised image was popularised by poets, painters, and musicians, making it a desirable destination for visitors seeking to discover Europe's "true heart."

The advent of river cruising in the late twentieth century, fuelled by technical advances in ship design, made these voyages more pleasant and accessible to a broader variety of travellers. Rhine cruises differ from other river excursions in that they combine breathtaking natural beauty with in-depth historical and cultural exploration. Along its banks, visitors may see everything from ancient Roman remains and Gothic churches to charming towns and world-renowned wineries.

Today, Rhine River cruises are especially important as a doorway to the core of European culture and history. The river flows through some of Germany, France, the Netherlands, and Switzerland's most distinctive areas, providing a distinct combination of art, architecture, gastronomy, and local customs. For many travellers, a Rhine cruise is more than simply a gorgeous voyage; it's an opportunity to connect with the rich history that has defined Europe for millennia.

As one begins on a Rhine River tour, it is difficult not to recognise the river's eternal importance. From ancient Romans to current travellers, the Rhine continues to fascinate and enthral people who travel along its historic route.

It is the best time to cruise.

The optimum time to take a Rhine River cruise is mainly determined by the kind of experience you want. The natural splendour and cultural treasures of the Rhine may be experienced all year, but the seasons bring distinct atmospheres, temperatures, and unique activities that can influence your trip.

Spring (April-June)

Spring is one of the most popular periods to sail the Rhine and with good reason. As the environment comes alive with flowering flowers, the vineyards and hills around the river become lush and colourful. The warm temperatures make it ideal for touring, discovering communities, and participating in outdoor sports. In early spring, the crowds are less, making for a more personal encounter. This time of year was especially good for walking tours and castle visits since the weather was pleasant but not scorching.

Summer (July-August)

Summer brings long, sunny days, making it an ideal time to relax on your cruise ship's outside decks and take in the breathtaking scenery. During this season, many villages and cities along the Rhine conduct festivals and activities. There's always something going on, from wine festivals in the villages to vibrant street markets. However, summer is the biggest season for Rhine cruises, so anticipate more people, particularly at famous ports such as Cologne and Strasbourg. If you prefer a vibrant environment and don't mind the busier season, summer is an excellent time to cruise.

Autumn (September-October)

Autumn is often considered the greatest season to sail the Rhine, and it was my favourite. The vineyards that flank the river change gold, red and orange, producing a stunning display of autumn colours. Autumn is also harvest season in the wine areas, thus there are several wine-tasting events and festivals. The colder weather provides for enjoyable days of touring, and the crowds are less than during the summer. It's the ideal season for those looking for a combination of breathtaking landscapes, cultural events, and a slower pace.

Winter (November-December)

While winter may seem to be a strange season to cruise, it is a lovely experience, particularly if you like Christmas markets. The Rhine's riverfront villages and cities come alive with festive decorations, dazzling lights, and quaint marketplaces selling local crafts, mulled wine, and Christmas goodies. Winter cruises often centre on Christmas markets, notably in Cologne, Rüdesheim, and Strasbourg. Although the weather might be frigid, there's something magical about visiting these holiday markets along the river. Winter cruises are also less crowded and more economical, providing a cosy and unique vacation experience.

Chapter 2. Plan Your Rhine River Journey

Choosing the Right Cruise Line

Choosing the correct cruise company is one of the most critical considerations you'll make when arranging your Rhine River trip. Each cruise company provides a distinct experience, ranging from luxury to more affordable, with a variety of facilities, activities, and itineraries. Here's a guide to choosing the cruise company that best suits your interests and travel style.

Determine Your Budget

River cruises along the Rhine may vary from economical to opulent, so determine a budget before looking into cruise possibilities. Some cruise lines provide all-inclusive packages that include meals, drinks, excursions, and gratuities; others charge for these items individually. If you like a hassle-free trip, an all-inclusive cruise may be the way to go; but, if you're on a tight budget, seek cruise lines that provide flexibility and enable you to pay just for what you need.

Choose the kind of experience you want

River cruise companies cater to a variety of travellers, so it's important to match your expectations with the appropriate cruise style. Here are a few popular categories:

• Luxury Cruises: If you want a high-end experience, look into luxury cruise lines like Viking River Cruises, AmaWaterways, or Crystal River Cruises. These cruise lines have large rooms, good meals, excellent service, and carefully chosen shore activities. They also prefer to have smaller ships that provide more personalised encounters.

• Cultural and Immersive Experiences: For travellers looking to immerse themselves in local culture and history, cruise companies such as Tauck or Uniworld Boutique River Cruises provide in-depth tours, local experts, and culturally enriching experiences. These lines aim to provide passengers with a real connection to the locations they visit.

• Family-Friendly Cruises: If you're travelling with kids or many generations, seek cruise lines that cater to families. AmaWaterways, for example, provides select family-oriented itineraries in collaboration with Disney's Adventures by Disney, which include kid-friendly excursions and activities suitable for all ages.

• Budget-Friendly Cruises: If you want to experience the Rhine River without breaking the bank, companies like Avalon Waterways or Scenic offer less expensive choices while still delivering good service, comfortable lodgings, and entertaining shore excursions. These brands often provide excellent value for money, striking a balance between price and enjoyment.

Review the Itineraries.

Each cruise operator provides various Rhine River itineraries, so select one that suits your interests. Some itineraries highlight large cities like Amsterdam, Cologne, and Strasbourg, while others include additional stops in smaller towns and villages, allowing you to discover hidden jewels along the river. Consider which sites are a must-see for you, such as the renowned Middle Rhine castles or the attractive wine villages of Alsace.

Also, examine the cruise's length. Shorter cruises (4-7 days) usually concentrate on a single stretch of the river, whilst longer cruises (10-14 days) provide a more thorough voyage that may include other rivers like the Main or the Moselle.

Onboard Amenities and Activities

The onboard facilities and activities differ amongst cruise lines. If you want a more active vacation, several cruise companies provide bicycles for rental at different ports, guided hiking trips, and even aboard fitness centres and wellness programs. AmaWaterways, for example, is well-known for its emphasis on health and wellbeing, with activities including yoga, fitness courses, and shore excursions on bikes.

If you like a more leisurely experience, select a line that emphasises relaxation and luxury. Many luxury cruise lines provide spa facilities, onboard entertainment such as classical music concerts, and wine or culinary excursions that provide a flavour of the locations you're visiting.

Consider the size of the ship.

River cruise ships are generally smaller than ocean liners, although their size varies. Larger ships may have more facilities, such as more dining choices and more public places, but smaller ships can give a more private and personal experience, with fewer passengers and a greater crew-to-passenger ratio. Whether you like a communal or private setting, the size of the ship may impact your decision.

Read reviews and do your research

Before making a final selection, check feedback from previous travellers. Websites such as TripAdvisor, Cruise Critic, and travel blogs may give valuable information on the overall experience, service quality, and excursions provided by various cruise companies. Don't simply look at the overall scores; go further into individual factors that are important to you, such as eating, service, and excursion quality.

Budgeting for Your Trip

Planning a Rhine River cruise requires careful planning to make the most of your trip without overpaying. Many factors influence the cost of a cruise, including shore excursions, food, and additional activities. Here's a tip to help you budget for your Rhine River trip.

Cruise fare

The majority of your cash will most likely go towards cruise cost, which varies greatly based on the cruise line, stateroom type, time of year, and duration of the trip. Luxury cruises are inherently more expensive, with all-inclusive services and high-end facilities, whilst more affordable choices may provide basic lodgings with optional extras. A 7-10 day Rhine River cruise typically costs between $1,500 and $6,000 per person.

• Luxury Cruises: Expect to pay between $3,000 and $6,000 per person for all-inclusive excursions with top amenities.

• Mid-vary Cruises: Prices for more typical alternatives may vary from $1,800 to $3,000 per person, which frequently includes certain meals and excursions.

• Budget Cruises: Basic cruises or last-minute discounts may cost as little as $1,500 per person, but facilities and inclusions will be restricted.

Cabin Type

The cabin you pick might significantly affect your entire cost. Most river cruise ships have a choice of accommodation options, ranging from modest cabins with tiny windows to suites with private balconies. Suites are more spacious and have nicer vistas, but they are also more expensive.

• Standard Cabins: Often the least expensive choice, these cabins are pleasant but may have fewer windows or no balcony. If you're on a tight budget and want to spend most of your time exploring, this might be an excellent method to save money.

• Balcony or Suite Cabins: If having a view of the Rhine from your lodging is important, upgrading to a balcony cabin or suite will increase your cost but may improve your experience, particularly in attractive places like the Middle Rhine Valley.

Seasonality

The time of year you select to cruise has a significant impact on the cost. High season (usually during the summer months) is more costly owing to increased demand, but shoulder seasons (spring and autumn) provide reduced costs while still providing great weather and fewer people. Winter cruises, particularly around Christmas markets, might provide reduced tickets but with cooler temperatures.

• High Season (July-August): Fares and demand are higher, so book well in advance.

• Shoulder Season (April-June, September-October): Prices are cheaper, and the weather is warm, ideal for avoiding peak-season crowds.

• Low Season (November-December): For those interested in Christmas market cruises, this is a more affordable season, but with cooler weather and fewer on-board activities.

Shore Excursions

Most river cruises include some basic shore excursions in their ticket, but many also offer extra trips and activities for an additional fee. These may include guided city tours, wine tastings, and castle visits, as well as more intensive activities like culinary courses or bike trips. The cost of these trips might vary, so plan appropriately.

• Basic Excursions: Frequently included in the cost, such as walking tours of major attractions or bus excursions.

• Optional Excursions: Prices vary from $50 to $200 per person, depending on the activity. Consider which trips are a must-do for you and budget accordingly.

Meals & Dining

While most cruise lines include meals in their rates, not all meals or dining experiences are included. Many cruises provide gourmet cuisine as part of the package, although speciality restaurants, beverages, or meals off the ship on excursions may incur an additional fee.

• All-Inclusive Cruises: All meals, including gourmet alternatives, and drinks (alcoholic and non-alcoholic), may be included, making it simpler to stay under budget.

• Standard Cruises: Some drinks and meals may be extra, particularly alcoholic beverages or eating at onboard speciality restaurants.

• Dining During Excursions: If you want to dine at local restaurants during your port calls, put up a separate budget for these meals.

Gratuities

Gratuities are a crucial part of your cruise budget that may sometimes be forgotten. Some cruise lines include gratuities in their prices, while others require you to pay crew members and guides after your voyage. To minimise surprises, be sure to verify whether gratuities are included.

• Included Gratuities: On luxury cruises, gratuities may be included in the package.

• Tipping: If not included, set aside $10-$15 per day per passenger for tips.

Travel insurance

Purchasing travel insurance is strongly advised for any cruise, particularly if you are travelling overseas. It protects against unexpected events like travel cancellations, medical problems, and misplaced baggage. Travel insurance normally costs between 4% and 10% of the overall trip cost, depending on the coverage.

Pre• and post-cruise expenses

If you want to spend extra time in towns like Amsterdam or Basel, which are often used as beginning or stopping places for Rhine cruises, keep in mind the expense of additional hotels, food, and sightseeing excursions. Allow for a couple nights in motels, meals at local restaurants, and transportation to and from the cruise port.

• Hotels: Depending on the city, hotel rates might range from $100 to $300 per night.

• Meals and Local Tours: Make a separate budget for meals and any sightseeing you want to undertake before or after your cruise.

Souvenirs and shopping

Don't forget to budget for souvenirs and any shopping you may do along the trip. It's worth saving aside modest money for vacation memories, such as wine from a Rhine winery, local crafts, or trinkets from the Christmas markets.

Packing Essentials for a River Cruise

Packing for a river trip involves careful planning to ensure that you are prepared for a wide range of activities, temperatures, and settings. Unlike ocean cruises, river cruises often entail smaller ships, more intimate settings, and numerous stops in towns and cities, so pack light but smart. Here's a list of the basics for your Rhine River cruise.

Comfortable Clothing

When preparing for a river trip, comfort is essential. You'll spend a lot of time seeing towns, going through historic sites, and even hiking or bicycling, so bring adaptable, comfortable attire.

• Casual Daywear: Pack lightweight, breathable clothes for everyday trips. Comfortable trousers or shorts, t-shirts and casual tops are great for sightseeing and walking trips. Layering is essential, particularly in spring and autumn when temperatures fluctuate throughout the day.

• Activewear: If your cruise itinerary includes bicycling tours, hiking excursions, or other physical activities, bring moisture-wicking clothing, comfy leggings or shorts, and supportive shoes.

• Smart Casual Evening Wear: Many river cruises have a casual dress code even for evening meals, while others may offer a more formal night or captain's dinner. Pack a couple of smart-casual ensembles, including a dress or blouse for ladies and trousers or a collared shirt for men.

Comfortable walking shoes

You'll most certainly spend a lot of time walking on beach excursions, so bring comfortable shoes.

• Walking Shoes: Choose durable, supportive shoes or trainers that can withstand cobblestone streets, rough terrain and long hours on your feet.

• Sandals or Slip-ons: A pair of comfy sandals or slip-on shoes for casual use on the ship or short trips around town is a nice touch.

Outerwear for Different Weather

The weather by the Rhine varies depending on the season, so always be prepared for colder temperatures or unexpected showers.

• Light Jacket or Sweater: On chilly nights or early mornings, a light jacket or sweater is required. If you're travelling in the shoulder seasons (spring or autumn), you may wish to pack a larger layer.

• Rain Gear: Bring a compact rain jacket or poncho, particularly if you're travelling in the spring or autumn when rains are more common. A compact travel umbrella is especially useful for unexpected weather outings.

• Scarf or Wrap: A multipurpose scarf or wrap may give warmth on colder days and is simple to transport.

Swimwear

While river cruise ships are typically smaller than ocean liners, they often have onboard amenities such as a pool or hot tub. If you want to use these facilities, be sure you carry a swimsuit.

• Swimsuit: Pack a swimsuit to relax in the onboard pool or hot tub.

• Cover-up: A light cover-up is recommended for strolling to and from the pool area.

Travel Accessories

A few useful travel gadgets can help make your voyage more comfortable and pleasant.

• Daypack or Crossbody Bag: For day trips, bring a compact, lightweight backpack or crossbody bag to hold basics like a water bottle, sunscreen, camera, and guidebook.

• Reusable Water Bottle: Staying hydrated throughout your tours is critical, so pack a reusable water bottle that can be filled on the ship and your excursions.

• Sunglasses and Hat: Wear a wide-brimmed hat and polarised sunglasses to protect yourself from the sun, particularly while touring outdoor attractions or lounging on the ship's sundeck.

Travel documents

You'll need to have all of your travel papers ready, particularly if your cruise schedule takes you through many countries.

• Passport: Make sure your passport is current and valid for at least six months after your travel.

• Travel Insurance paperwork: Keep a copy of your travel insurance policy and any other necessary paperwork for your trip.

• Cruise and airline Tickets: Print or preserve digital copies of your cruise and airline tickets, as well as any hotel bookings if you want to stay before or after your cruise.

Toiletries and medication

While most cruise ships supply basic amenities, it's a good idea to carry your own, particularly if you use any specific goods on a regular basis.

• Travel-sized Toiletries: Bring travel-sized shampoo, conditioner, body wash, and lotion. Don't forget about additional personal care supplies like toothpaste, deodorant, and a razor.

• prescriptions: Bring enough prescription prescriptions to last the whole trip, as well as any over-the-counter medications you may need, such as pain relievers, allergy medication, or motion sickness pills.

• Sunscreen and Lip Balm: Use sunscreen and SPF lip balm to protect your skin from the sun when on excursions and deck.

Electronics and chargers

You'll most certainly want to record memories and remain connected on your trip, so don't forget your necessary devices and chargers.

• Camera or Smartphone: Whether you're a seasoned photographer or prefer to use your phone, bring your camera or smartphone to capture the gorgeous landscape and historic monuments along the Rhine.

• Portable Charger: A portable charger might come in useful on extended trips when power outlets may not be available.

• Plug adaptor: Depending on where your cruise leaves from, you may need a power adaptor for European outlets. Most Rhine river cruises travel through Germany, France, and the Netherlands, thus a Type C or Type F adaptor is necessary.

Reading material or entertainment

While river cruises include a variety of activities, you may wish to bring a book or e-reader to enjoy during calmer times on board.

• Books or e-Reader: Bring a novel, guidebook, or e-reader to read while resting on the ship's deck or in your stateroom.

• diary: Consider packing a trip diary to record noteworthy events, recommendations, and notes about the places you visit.

Miscellaneous

A few more things might improve your river trip experience:

• Binoculars: Ideal for admiring magnificent vistas or spotting animals as you cruise through breathtaking settings.

• Travel Laundry Kit: Some travellers prefer to carry light and wash laundry on the go. A compact washing kit with detergent and a mobile clothesline will allow you to wash clothing in your cabin.

Chapter 3. Popular Rhine River Cruise Routes

Northbound versus Southbound Itineraries

When arranging a Rhine River cruise, one of the most important choices you'll make is whether to go northbound or southbound. Both ways include breathtaking scenery, historical sites, and lovely villages, but the experience varies somewhat depending on which direction you go down the river. Here's an overview of what to anticipate from each route to help you select the one that best meets your needs.

Northbound itineraries

A northbound itinerary often begins in Switzerland, near the city of Basel, and proceeds down the Rhine River to the Netherlands, frequently terminating in Amsterdam. This route provides a gentle transition from Switzerland's alpine, picturesque grandeur to Germany and the Netherlands' flatter landscapes and cultural centres.

Key highlights of a northbound journey:

• Swiss Alps and Basel: If you go to Switzerland, you will begin your tour under the shadow of the beautiful Alps, taking in the fresh air and stunning mountain vistas. Basel, a cultural hotspot with a historic old town and art museums, is an excellent destination to visit before boarding your cruise.

• Middle Rhine Gorge: As you go north, you'll pass through the UNESCO-designated Middle Rhine Gorge, which is known for its stunning cliffs, vineyards, and mediaeval castles situated on hilltops. This portion is a highlight of the voyage, with some of the most famous vistas of the Rhine.

• German Cities and Towns: Northbound itineraries often include stops in ancient German cities like as Koblenz, where the Rhine joins the Moselle River, and Cologne, which is famous for its tall Gothic cathedral. You'll also visit smaller towns such as Rüdesheim, known for its wine, and Heidelberg, which has a lovely castle and Germany's oldest university.

• Amsterdam and Dutch Canals: The voyage ends at Amsterdam, a city famous for its network of gorgeous canals, thriving art scene, and historic sites. The Netherlands' flat landscapes give a contrast to the hilly areas earlier in the tour, resulting in a serene and picturesque conclusion to your voyage.

Why Choose a Northbound Itinerary?

• Mountainous Start: Starting your journey in Switzerland's Alpine beauty provides an unforgettable introduction to the Rhine.

• Gradual Transition: As you travel north, the landscapes grow less harsh, creating a pleasing visual transition from stunning mountains to the tranquil lowlands of the Netherlands.

• End in Amsterdam: Amsterdam's rich culture and history, together with its excellent transit connections, make it an ideal site to explore more or start your journey home.

Southbound itineraries

A southbound itinerary often begins in Amsterdam and follows the Rhine River upstream to Switzerland. This route provides a unique view of the river's scenery and towns as you sail towards the Rhine's source in the Swiss Alps.

Key highlights of a southbound journey:

• Amsterdam's Vibrant Culture: Begin your journey in the busy and culturally rich city of Amsterdam, where you may visit its numerous museums, historic buildings, and renowned canals. It's a boisterous start that sets the tone for the remainder of the journey.

• German Castles and Villages: As you sail southward, you'll travel through the heart of Germany, with frequent pauses at the Middle Rhine Gorge, home to stunning castles and the famed Lorelei Rock. You'll see places like Speyer, noted for its majestic cathedral, and Strasbourg, which combines French and German elements.

• Swiss Conclusion: The voyage ends at Basel, a Swiss city famed for its thriving art scene, mediaeval old town, and closeness to the Alps. From here, you may continue your journey and visit Switzerland's famed alpine villages like Lucerne, or take a picturesque train ride to the summit of the Jungfraujoch.

• Heidelberg and Koblenz: On your trip upstream, take in the delightful old-world ambience of Heidelberg, one of Germany's most attractive cities, and Koblenz, home to the famous Ehrenbreitstein Fortress.

Why Choose a Southbound Itinerary?

• City Start: Amsterdam has a plethora of sights to discover before you take sail. It is also a significant international centre, which makes it handy for visitors.

• Dramatic Finale in the Alps: Concluding your voyage in Switzerland means ending on a high note, with views of the breathtaking Swiss Alps and the option to prolong your journey to one of Europe's most picturesque nations.

• Upstream Experience: As you go south against the flow of the river, you can see the sceneries increase to greater heights, culminating in Switzerland's alpine splendour.

Key differences between northbound and southbound

• Starting Point: Northbound voyages begin in Switzerland, with an early emphasis on alpine landscapes, whilst southbound cruises begin in Amsterdam, with a focus on the Netherlands' cultural riches.

• Ending Point: Northbound excursions often terminate in Amsterdam, whilst southbound itineraries end in Basel or another Swiss city, perhaps providing access to Switzerland's magnificent landscapes at the conclusion of your journey.

• Flow of Landscapes: Northbound cruises go from alpine Switzerland to flatter, more pastoral areas, and southbound cruises give the opposite experience, building up to magnificent Alpine panoramas.

Which Itinerary Is Right For You?

Choosing a northern or southbound Rhine River cruise is based on your specific travel preferences:

• If you prefer to begin your adventure in the breathtaking Swiss Alps and gradually sail towards the flatlands and cultural liveliness of the Netherlands, a northbound route may be the best option.

• If you want to begin in the Netherlands, see Amsterdam's rich history, and leave the mountain splendour of Switzerland for the spectacular conclusion, a southbound itinerary may be more tempting.

Both approaches provide equally rich cultural experiences, breathtaking scenery, and unique opportunities to discover Europe's history and charm. Whatever you select, your Rhine River cruise will be an unforgettable experience.

Customise Your Cruise Experience

One of the most appealing parts of a Rhine River cruise is the ability to tailor to your interests, tastes, and travel style. Whether you're an explorer looking for off-the-beaten-path adventures, a history buff looking for cultural enrichment, or a gourmet in search of local cuisine, you can tailor your cruise to your exact specifications. Here are some ideas to personalise your Rhine River boat experience.

Choose the Right Type of Cruise

The first step in personalising your vacation is to choose a cruise that suits your interests. There are various sorts of cruises offered on the Rhine River, each with a unique theme and focus:

• Cultural Cruises: These cruises highlight the Rhine Valley's rich history and tradition. You will get the chance to visit museums, explore mediaeval castles, and take guided tours of ancient cities such as Cologne, Strasbourg, and Heidelberg.

• Wine and Gastronomy Cruises: Ideal for food and wine enthusiasts, these cruises take you through the Rhine Valley, where you may sample wine at local wineries, eat regional cuisine, and participate in onboard cooking lessons.

• Active and Adventure Cruises: For those seeking a more active experience, several cruise companies offer adventure-themed itineraries such as bicycle tours, hiking excursions through gorgeous vineyards, and guided kayaking expeditions down the river.

• Holiday Cruises: If you want to experience the charm of European Christmas markets, a holiday-themed cruise in December includes festive stops in locations such as Rüdesheim and Cologne, where you can visit traditional markets, drink mulled wine, and shop for unique presents.

Choose the Right Excursions.

Most river cruises provide a range of shore excursions at each stop, allowing you to choose activities that interest you. Some cruise companies even let you create your schedule by choosing from a variety of excursion options:

- Historical Tours: Discover the old Roman history of places such as Koblenz or stroll through the cobblestone lanes of mediaeval villages. Along the Rhine Gorge, visitors may see centuries-old castles, Gothic cathedrals, and UNESCO World Heritage sites.

- Wine and Vineyard excursions: If you like wine, consider vineyard excursions and tastings in places such as Rüdesheim and Bacharach. Learn about the region's winemaking traditions and try some world-class Rieslings.

- Nature Excursions: Nature enthusiasts may enjoy a refreshing outdoor experience by hiking or cycling through the magnificent vistas of the Black Forest or the terraced vineyards of the Rhine Valley.

- Custom Excursions: Some cruise companies even enable you to book customised, tailor-made excursions to see certain locations, museums, or activities that are not included in normal itineraries.

Choose themed cruises or special events.

Many cruise companies provide themed cruises, allowing passengers to engage in specialised interests or seasonal activities. Choosing a themed cruise allows you to personalise your experience.

- Wine Harvest Cruises: If you visit during the grape harvest season (late summer or early autumn), you may choose between cruises that highlight the region's winemaking traditions. These cruises feature vineyard excursions, wine tastings, and discussions about the winemaking process.

- Christmas Market Cruises: For a spectacular holiday experience, book a Christmas market cruise in late November or December. You'll visit some of Europe's most renowned markets, including those in Cologne, Koblenz, and Strasbourg, where you can buy handcrafted presents, taste festive sweets, and soak in the holiday spirit.

- Art and Culture Cruises: For art aficionados, several cruises offer unique art-themed voyages that include museum tours, art workshops, and performances celebrating the Rhine region's diverse cultural legacy.

Personalise your onboarding experience.

Aside from shore activities, you may tailor your cruise experience to your preferences. Many river cruise operators provide a range of methods to personalise your sailing experience:

- Dining Preferences: If you have unique dietary requirements or preferences, most cruise lines can accommodate vegetarian, vegan, gluten-free, or other dietary restrictions. Some cruises also offer regional cuisine evenings, when you may sample meals from the locations you're visiting.

- Room Upgrades: For increased comfort, you may choose from a choice of cabin types, including conventional river-view cabins and more deluxe suites with private balconies. Some cabins even provide personalised amenities and improved services.

- Private Events: Some cruise companies enable you to plan private events aboard, such as a special supper with friends or a commemoration of a significant birthday or anniversary.

Add pre-or post-cruise extensions.

Many cruise companies provide pre- or post-cruise extensions, which enable you to spend extra time in significant destinations at the start or finish of your voyage. You may tailor these extensions to your interests:

• Explore Switzerland: If your cruise starts or finishes in Basel, consider staying longer to see Lucerne, Zurich, or the Swiss Alps. You may take a scenic train trip to the summit of a mountain or see Switzerland's picturesque lakes and towns.

• Discover the Netherlands: If your cruise begins or ends in Amsterdam, you may extend your stay to see the city's museums, canals, and bustling neighbourhoods. You might also plan a day excursion to neighbouring sights such as Keukenhof Gardens or the Windmills of Zaanse Schans.

• Explore More of Germany or France: Extend your cruise by visiting Heidelberg, Strasbourg, or even Paris to get a better understanding of the surrounding areas.

Customise Your Cruise to Your Interests and Group.

If you're travelling with a group of family or friends, you may tailor your cruise to their interests and dynamics:

• Multi-Generational Cruises: Some cruise lines include activities and excursions tailored to travellers of all ages, making them suitable for multi-generational journeys. You may choose family-friendly activities or arrange adjoining cabins for more convenient lodging.

• lone Traveler alternatives: Many cruise lines provide reduced prices for lone travellers and arrange social activities or group dining alternatives to enable solo cruisers to meet other passengers.

Chapter 4. Top destinations and stopovers

Amsterdam, Netherlands: Gateway to the Rhine

Amsterdam, the vibrant capital of the Netherlands, is frequently the starting point for many Rhine River cruises, serving as the "Gateway to the Rhine." Known for its picturesque canals, historic architecture, and rich cultural scene, Amsterdam provides travellers with an ideal blend of exploration and relaxation before embarking on their voyage. Whether you spend a few days in Amsterdam before or after your cruise, there are plenty of sights and activities to enjoy.

What to Explore in Amsterdam

Amsterdam is a city that appeals to all sorts of visitors, with world-class museums, beautiful neighbourhoods, and vibrant marketplaces. Here are a few must-see attractions:

Rijksmuseum

The Rijksmuseum, one of Amsterdam's most recognised cultural icons, is home to a vast collection of Dutch classics, including works by Rembrandt and Vermeer. The museum provides a thorough exploration of Dutch history and art, making it a must-see for cultural fans.

Anne Frank's House

This historic museum depicts the heartbreaking tale of Anne Frank, a Jewish girl who fled from the Nazis during World War II. Located in the home where she penned her famous diary, the museum provides an emotional and instructive experience.

Van Gogh Museum

Art aficionados should not miss the Van Gogh Museum, which houses the world's biggest collection of Vincent van Gogh's masterpieces. Visitors may see iconic artworks like "Sunflowers" and "The Bedroom."

Canal cruises

A picturesque boat excursion allows you to see Amsterdam's famed canals. You'll float by historic houses, bridges, and sites while learning about the city's maritime heritage. Evening excursions provide an especially magnificent perspective of the city, as the canals are lit.

The Jordaan District

The Jordaan is a lovely and scenic neighbourhood noted for its tiny alleyways, cafés, and shops, making it ideal for a leisurely walk. You may explore local markets like Noordermarkt or relax with a cup of coffee at a cosy café.

Vondelpark

If you're searching for a calm escape from the city, Vondelpark provides a beautiful green environment for a stroll, picnic, or bike ride. It's an excellent place to relax and people-watch before boarding your cruise.

The Heineken Experience

Beer fans may visit the Heineken brewery and participate in the interactive Heineken Experience. This tour includes an overview of the brewing process and, of course, some sampling along the way.

Bloemenmarkt

Bloemenmarkt, the world's first floating flower market, is a vivid and colourful location to explore. It's the ideal place to get tulip bulbs and other Dutch flowers.

How to Get to Amsterdam

By Air

Amsterdam is serviced by Amsterdam Schiphol Airport (AMS), one of Europe's busiest and best-connected airports. Many overseas locations provide direct flights to Schiphol Airport. The airport is about a 20-minute rail or taxi ride from the city centre.

• From airport to city centre:

The train from Schiphol Airport to Amsterdam Central Station operates regularly and takes approximately 15-20 minutes. You may also take a cab or a shuttle, but the train is usually the quickest and least expensive choice.

By train

If you are already in Europe, travelling to Amsterdam by rail is a practical choice. The city has excellent connections to major European cities via high-speed rail networks such as the Thalys and Eurostar. For example:

• From Paris, the Thalys high-speed train takes around 3 hours and 20 minutes to reach Amsterdam.

• From Brussels, the Thalys provides a direct train to Amsterdam in about 2 hours.

by car

If you prefer to drive, Amsterdam has excellent road connections to neighbouring countries. However, parking in the city may be costly, and traffic can be congested, so consider leaving your vehicle at a park-and-ride facility outside the city centre.

By bus

Several bus operators, including FlixBus, provide economical trips from several European towns to Amsterdam. While bus travel takes longer than trains or aircraft, it might be a more affordable choice for budget travellers.

Cost of Exploring Amsterdam

Amsterdam is typically regarded as a relatively costly city, particularly in terms of lodging and food. Here is a general estimate of the prices for a day of sightseeing in Amsterdam.

• Accommodation

- Budget Hotels/Hostels: €50 to €100 per night
- Mid-range hotels: €120 to €200 per night.
- Luxury hotels cost more than €250 per night.
- Food&Dining:
- A budget dinner at a nearby café costs between €10 and €15.
- Mid-range restaurant meal: €20 to €40 per person.
- Fine dinner experience costs €60+ per person.
- transport:
- Public transport (tram, bus, metro): €3.40 for a one-hour ticket
- Day passes are €8.50 for 24 hours.
- Bike rental: €10 to €15 per day.
- Entry Fees for Major Attractions
- Rijksmuseum admission: €20.
- Anne Frank House, €14.
- Van Gogh Museum: €20.
- Canal cruise costs €15-€25.

Cologne, Germany: The Iconic Cathedral and Historic Sites

Cologne, one of Germany's oldest and greatest cities, is an essential stop on every Rhine River cruise. Cologne, known for its famous Cologne Cathedral, beautiful Old Town, and rich history, provides tourists with a unique combination of historical depth and contemporary energy. The city, located on the Rhine River, has long been a major cultural and trade centre in Germany, making it an ideal stopover for visitors looking to experience both its old and modern attractions.

What to Explore in Cologne

Cologne Cathedral (Kölner Dom).

The towering Cologne Cathedral, a UNESCO World Heritage Site, is the city's most recognisable feature. This Gothic masterpiece took more than 600 years to create and is known for its twin spires that dominate the skyline. Visitors may tour the spectacular interior, enjoy the exquisite stained-glass windows, and climb the 533 steps to the South Tower for panoramic views of the city and the Rhine River.

Old Town (Altstadt)

Cologne's Old Town is a quaint tangle of tiny, cobblestone alleyways surrounded by colourful ancient structures. You may tour charming squares like Alter Markt and Heumarkt, and eat traditional German food at one of the numerous outdoor cafés or beer gardens. The Old Town also houses some of Cologne's most significant churches, including St. Martin's Church and Gross St. Martin are worth a visit.

The Roman-Germanic Museum (Römisch-Germanisches Museum)

Cologne's Roman legacy is on exhibit in the Roman-Germanic Museum, which is near the cathedral. The museum houses intriguing artefacts from the city's past as a Roman colony, such as mosaics, sculptures, and daily objects. One of the standouts is the well-preserved Dionysus Mosaic from a Roman villa.

The Hohenzollern Bridge

The Hohenzollern Bridge is one of Cologne's most recognisable landmarks, known for the hundreds of "love locks" fastened to it by couples from all over the globe. The bridge provides excellent views of the Rhine and the Cathedral, particularly around sunset, making it a favourite picture location.

Cologne Chocolate Museum (Schokoladenmuseum Köln).

The Cologne Chocolate Museum provides a pleasant and tasty stop for tourists of all ages, taking them on a trip through the history of chocolate making. You may see chocolate being created, learn about the history of cocoa, and, of course, try some delicious goodies.

Kölsch Beer and Brauhaus Culture

Cologne is known for its Kölsch beer, a light, crisp beer served in small glasses known as "Stangen." A visit to one of Cologne's traditional Brauhauses (breweries) is a must, where you can try fresh Kölsch and enjoy hearty local dishes like Himmel und Ääd (potatoes, apples and black pudding).

Museum Ludwig

Art aficionados should visit the Museum Ludwig, which has one of Europe's most significant collections of contemporary art. The museum's collection includes pieces by Picasso, Warhol, and Lichtenstein, as well as modern German artists.

The Rhine Promenade

For a stroll, visit the Rhine Promenade, where you can walk along the river and enjoy breathtaking views of the city. The promenade is also an excellent place to enjoy a boat trip down the Rhine.

How To Get To Cologne

By Air

Cologne is serviced by Cologne Bonn Airport (CGN), which is about 15 kilometres southeast of the city centre. The airport serves both international and local flights, making it an ideal entrance point for travellers.

• From airport to city centre:

The S-Bahn (S13 or S19) trains go straight from the airport to Cologne Central Station (Köln Hauptbahnhof). The travel takes around 15 minutes and costs roughly €3. Alternatively, you may take a cab for about €30.

By train

Cologne is a significant hub in the European rail network, with high-speed trains like the ICE and Thalys connecting it to other cities.

• From Amsterdam, direct trains take around 2 hours and 40 minutes.

• From Frankfurt, take the ICE train to Cologne in roughly one hour.

by car

Major roads connect Cologne to other German and European cities, making it conveniently accessible by vehicle. However, parking in the city centre might be pricey, so consider using public transit when you arrive.

By bus

Several low-cost bus services, such as FlixBus, provide trips to Cologne from several European cities. While bus travel is slower than trains or planes, it might be a cheaper choice.

Cost of Exploring Cologne

Cologne has a variety of experiences to suit various budgets. Here's a breakdown of the estimated prices for a day in the city:

• **Accommodation**

• Budget hotels/hostels: €50 to €90 per night.

• Mid-range hotels cost €100-€150 per night.

- Luxury hotels cost over €200 per night.

- **Food&Dining:**

- A budget dinner at a neighbourhood café or food stall costs between €8 and €15.

- Mid-range restaurant: €20–€35 per person.

- Fine dinner costs above €50 per person.

- **transport:**

- A single public transport ticket (tram, bus, or train) costs €3.00.

A Day ticket for unlimited travel is €8.80.

- Taxi journeys inside the city start at €4, plus €1.80 per km.

- **Entry Fees for Major Attractions**

- Cologne Cathedral: Free (minor cost for tower climb, around €5).

- Roman-Germanic Museum: €6 to €10.

The Museum Ludwig costs €12.

- Chocolate Museum, €13.50.

- Guided walking tour of the Old Town: €15-€20.

Koblenz: The meeting of the Rhine and Moselle rivers

Koblenz is a lovely city at the junction of the Rhine and Moselle rivers, sometimes known as the Deutsches Eck (German Corner). Koblenz's strategic position has transformed it into a historic and cultural metropolis, complete with historical fortifications, beautiful squares, and picturesque riverbank vistas. As one of Germany's oldest towns, Koblenz combines mediaeval architecture with natural beauty.

What to Explore in Koblenz

Deutsche Eck (German Corner)

At the point where the Rhine and Moselle rivers meet, you'll discover the renowned Deutsches Eck, a landmark with an imposing equestrian monument of Emperor William I. The location provides panoramic views of both rivers and is a popular place to begin your trip.

Ehrenbreitstein Fortress

Perched high above the Rhine, the Ehrenbreitstein Fortress is one of Europe's biggest intact strongholds. You may get to the fortress by taking an exciting cable car journey over the Rhine, which provides breathtaking views of Koblenz. Once in the fortress, you may tour its expansive gardens, and museums, and learn about its military history.

Old Town (Altstadt)

Koblenz's Old Town is a lovely collection of small lanes, half-timbered homes, and ancient structures. Stroll around Am Plan, one of Koblenz's oldest squares, or see the Basilica of St. Castor, the city's oldest church, which was erected in the ninth century.

Koblenzer Cable Car

The Koblenz Cable Car transports you from the Rhine promenade to the Ehrenbreitstein Fortress. It's a thrilling way to observe the city from above, particularly around sunset. The journey offers stunning views of the Rhine-Moselle confluence.

The Schängelbrunnen Fountain

The Schängelbrunnen Fountain, located in the courtyard of the Town Hall, serves as a fun emblem of Koblenz. The bronze child spits water occasionally, making it a unique and entertaining stop when visiting the Old Town.

The Rhine Promenade

Take a stroll along the Rhine Promenade, where you can enjoy river vistas, passing ships, and the city's bustling ambience. The promenade is dotted with cafés and restaurants, ideal for a leisurely lunch or drink by the sea.

How To Get To Koblenz

By Air

The closest major airport to Koblenz is Frankfurt Airport (FRA), which is about 110 km away. From there, you may take a direct train or hire a vehicle to Koblenz.

• rail: The rail travel from Frankfurt Airport to Koblenz takes around 1 hour and 20 minutes and costs between €20 and €40, depending on the kind of train.

By train

Koblenz is well-connected by rail, with frequent connections to major German cities and neighbouring countries.

• From Frankfurt, direct trains take around one hour.

• From Cologne, a high-speed ICE train will take you to Koblenz in approximately one hour.

by car

The A3 and A61 highways connect Koblenz, making it easily accessible by vehicle. The travel from Frankfurt takes around 1.5 hours, whereas the drive from Cologne takes roughly an hour.

By boat

Koblenz is a popular stop on Rhine River excursions, with many passengers arriving by riverboat. The city's strategic position on the Rhine makes it a suitable port of call for both short and long-distance cruises.

The cost of exploring Koblenz

- **Accommodation**

- Budget: €50 to €80 per night

- Mid-range: €90–€150 each night.

- Luxury: more than €200 per night.

- **Dining:**

- Budget meal: €8–€15

- Mid-range restaurant: €20–€35 per person.

- Fine dinner costs above €50 per person.

- **transport:**

The local bus ticket is €2.50.

- Round-trip cable car prices range from €11 to €15.

- **Attraction:**

- Ehrenbreitstein Fortress (with cable car) costs €14.

- Deutsche Eck: Free.

- Old Town walking tours: €10 to €15 per person.

Rüdesheim: Wine Country Charm.

Rüdesheim, situated in the Rheingau wine region, is one of the most scenic villages along the Rhine River, with exquisite vineyards, mediaeval architecture, and a rich cultural past. Rüdesheim, a popular stop on Rhine River cruises, allows guests to experience both the beautiful grandeur of the Rhine Valley and the heritage of winemaking.

What to Explore in Rüdesheim

Drosselgasse

Rüdesheim's main street, Drosselgasse, is a bustling, small road dotted with historic wine bars, restaurants, and tourist stores. The atmosphere is lively, particularly in the evenings when live music fills the air. This old lane is the centre of Rüdesheim's wine culture.

The Rüdesheim Wine Museum

The Rüdesheim Wine Museum, located in the Brömserburg Castle, provides an overview of the Rheingau's centuries-old winemaking traditions. Visitors may learn about the history of wine production and taste local wines while admiring the breathtaking views of the Rhine.

Siegfried's Mechanical Music Cabinet

This unusual museum has a wonderful array of self-playing musical instruments from the past. The museum, housed in a mediaeval structure, provides an enjoyable and participatory experience for visitors of all ages.

The Niederwald Monument

The Niederwald Monument, which overlooks the town and Rhine Valley, is a must-see for its breathtaking panoramic views. A short cable car trip takes you above the vineyards to this historic monument commemorating Germany's unification in 1871.

Wine tasting and vineyard tours

The Rheingau area is renowned for its superb Riesling wines. Many local vineyards provide tastings and tours, allowing visitors to experience the region's greatest vintages while learning about the winemaking process. Don't pass up the opportunity to drink a glass of Riesling while admiring the views of the neighbouring vineyards.

River Cruises & Wine Tours

For a picturesque experience, take a boat cruise from Rüdesheim to adjacent towns and castles along the Rhine. Wine enthusiasts may also schedule a guided wine trip to visit different Rheingau estates.

How To Get To Rüdesheim

By Air

The nearest major airport is Frankfurt Airport (FRA), which is around 60 km from Rüdesheim. From the airport, you may take a direct rail or hire a vehicle to go to town.

• Train: The travel from Frankfurt to Rüdesheim takes around an hour and costs between €15 and €30.

By train

Rüdesheim is readily accessible by rail from major German cities.

• From Frankfurt: Direct trains operate frequently and take around one hour.

• From Cologne, a picturesque train trip down the Rhine takes around 1.5 to two hours.

by car

Rüdesheim is linked by the B42 road, which makes it accessible by automobile. The travel from Frankfurt takes around an hour, whereas the drive from Cologne takes about two hours.

By boat

Rüdesheim is a popular destination for Rhine River excursions, with several riverboats mooring here along the way. You may also take a local boat to adjacent Rhine towns.

Cost of exploring Rüdesheim

• **Accommodation**

• Budget: €60 to €90 per night

• Mid-range: €100–€150 each night.

• Luxury: more than €200 per night.

• **Dining:**

• Budget meal: €10 to €15

• Mid-range restaurant: €25 to €40 per person.

• Fine dinner costs above €50 per person.

• **transport:**

• Local bus ticket costs €2.50-€3.

• Cable car to Niederwald Monument: €10 to €15 (round trip).

• **Attraction:**

- Wine Museum: €6–€10.

- Siegfried's Mechanical Music Cabinet: €8–€10.

- Wine tasting tour: €10 to €20 per person.

Heidelberg: The Romantic City of Castles.

Heidelberg is known for its fairytale appeal, which is enhanced by the imposing Heidelberg Castle and the gorgeous background of the Neckar River and surrounding hills. Heidelberg is known as one of Germany's most romantic cities, with a rich history, culture, and natural beauty. With its cobblestone lanes, active university life, and ageless architecture, it's a must-see destination for every Rhine tourist.

What to Explore in Heidelberg

Heidelberg Castle

The city's greatest beauty, Heidelberg Castle, is a breathtaking combination of Gothic and Renaissance architecture. Perched on a hill above the Old Town and Neckar River, the castle provides beautiful views and the chance to explore its mediaeval ruins, gardens, and the legendary Heidelberg Tun, one of the world's biggest wine barrels. Entry to the castle includes entrance to the German Pharmacy Museum, which is located inside.

The Philosopher's Walk (Philosophenweg)

This lovely walking trail along the northern bank of the Neckar River offers panoramic views of Heidelberg Castle and the Old Town. It was previously a popular destination for philosophers and poets, who were inspired by the breathtaking views.

Heidelberg's Old Town (Altstadt)

Heidelberg's Altstadt is full of small alleyways, antique buildings, and attractive squares. Marktplatz, the centre plaza, is flanked by cafés and restaurants, and the magnificent Church of the Holy Spirit is adjacent. Another well-known landmark is the Old Bridge (Alte Brücke), which has mediaeval towers.

Heidelberg University

Heidelberg University is the oldest university in Germany, having been founded in 1386. Visitors may visit the historic campus, which includes the Studentenkarzer (Student Prison), where disobedient students were previously detained, and the University Library, which houses rare manuscripts.

Alte Brücke, or Old Bridge

This 18th-century stone bridge crosses the Neckar River, connecting Old Town to Philosopher's Walk. The bridge has lovely sculptures and provides stunning views of the castle and surrounding hills.

How To Get To Heidelberg

By Air

The closest major airport is Frankfurt Airport (FRA), which is about 80 km from Heidelberg. From the airport, you may take a direct rail or bus into the city.

• Train: The travel from Frankfurt Airport to Heidelberg takes around 50-60 minutes, and tickets range from €20 to €40.

By train

Heidelberg is well-linked to Germany's efficient rail network.

• From Frankfurt: Trains operate regularly and take around 50 minutes.

• From Stuttgart, a direct train to Heidelberg takes around one hour.

• The travel from Cologne takes around 2 hours by high-speed ICE train.

by car

Heidelberg is accessible by the A5 and A6 motorways. The travel from Frankfurt takes around an hour, while the trip from Stuttgart takes about 1.5 hours.

Cost of exploring Heidelberg

• Accommodation

• Budget: €60 to €90 per night

• Mid-range: €100–€150 each night.

• Luxury: more than €200 per night.

• Dining:

• Budget meal: €10 to €15

• Mid-range restaurant: €20–€35 per person.

• Fine dinner costs above €50 per person.

• transport:

• Local tram or bus ticket costs €2.50.

- Funicular to Heidelberg Castle: €9–€15 (round journey, including castle access)

- **Attraction:**

- Heidelberg Castle and Garden: €9

The Philosopher's Walk is free

- Heidelberg Tun: Free (included with castle ticket).

- Student Prison costs €3.

Strasbourg, France: A blend of French and German culture.

Strasbourg, situated near the German border in the Alsace region, has a distinct blend of French and German influences in its architecture, food, and culture. Strasbourg, the home of the European Parliament and a UNESCO World Heritage site, is a thriving city noted for its gorgeous half-timbered buildings, charming waterways, and rich history. It's a must-see for visitors looking to enjoy the finest of both French and German cultures.

What to Explore in Strasbourg

Strasbourg Cathedral (Cathedrale Notre-Dame)

The Strasbourg Cathedral is one of Europe's most spectacular Gothic cathedrals, distinguished by its tall spire, complex façade, and exquisite stained glass windows. Don't miss the astronomical clock inside, which attracts people every day at noon. Visitors may also climb to the summit to get panoramic views of the city.

La Petite France

The La Petite France quarter is Strasbourg's most picturesque, with meandering canals, cobblestone lanes, and mediaeval half-timbered buildings. This historic miller and fisherman's quarter is great for leisurely walks, photography, and finding charming cafés and stores.

Palais Rohan

This 18th-century palace has three museums: the Museum of Fine Arts, the Museum of Decorative Arts, and the Archaeological Museum. It is an excellent visit for history and art enthusiasts, providing insight into Strasbourg's regal past.

The European Parliament

The European Parliament is located in Strasbourg, and guided tours are available to learn about how the European Union works. The Parliament's modern architecture contrasts with Strasbourg's traditional appeal, making it an important cultural and political monument.

Boat tours on the Ill River

To view Strasbourg from a new perspective, take a boat tour down the Ill River, which encircles the city's historic centre. It's an excellent opportunity to see monuments like the Covered Bridges and Vauban Dam while learning about the city's history.

Alsatian Cuisine

Strasbourg cuisine is a lovely blend of French and German flavours. Local favourites include tarte flambée (akin to a thin pizza), choucroute garnie (sauerkraut with sausages and meats), and kougelhopf (a traditional cake).

How to Get to Strasbourg

By Air

The nearest airport is Strasbourg Airport (SXB), which is approximately 10 kilometres from the city centre. From the airport, you may take a rail or cab to the city in 15 minutes.

• Train: Tickets from the airport to the city centre cost around €4.

By train

Strasbourg is readily accessible by rail, having good links to France and Germany.

• From Paris: The high-speed TGV train takes around 2 hours and costs between €50 and €100.

• From Frankfurt: The train ride lasts around 2 hours and costs between €40 and €80.

by car

Strasbourg is well linked by roads, making it easily accessible by automobile from both France and Germany. The travel from Paris takes around 4.5 hours, while the drive from Frankfurt takes about 2.5 hours.

Cost of exploring Strasbourg

• **Accommodation**

• Budget: €60 to €90 per night

• Mid-range: €100–€150 each night.

• Luxury: more than €200 per night.

• **Dining:**

• Budget meal: €10 to €15

• Mid-range restaurant: €25 to €40 per person.

- Fine dinner costs above €50 per person.

- **transport:**

A Local tram or bus ticket costs €1.80.

- Boat tour: €10–€15.

- **Attraction:**

- Strasbourg Cathedral: Free (with an extra cost for the tower climb).

- Palais Rohan museums: €6 to €8 per museum.

- European Parliament: Free (with pre-booked tour).

Basel, Switzerland: The Journey Ends and Beyond

Basel, commonly the last destination on many Rhine River cruises, is a thriving cultural centre at the crossroads of Switzerland, Germany, and France. Basel, known for its mediaeval old town, world-class museums, and contemporary architecture, provides a unique combination of history, art, and innovation. The city's position on the Rhine and cosmopolitan culture make it ideal for exploring both the conclusion of your river voyage and what comes ahead.

What to Explore in Basel

Basel Minster (Basler Münster).

This distinctive red sandstone cathedral is a symbol of Basel, with a beautiful blend of Romanesque and Gothic architecture. Visitors may climb the towers to get panoramic views of the city and the Rhine River. The cathedral's stunning cloisters and historical importance make it a must-see.

Old Town (Altstadt)

Basel's Old Town is a lovely tangle of small alleyways adorned with mediaeval architecture, colourful fountains, and secret courtyards. Key locations include Marktplatz, which houses the imposing Basel Town Hall (Rathaus), and Spalenberg, which is noted for its boutique stores and cafés.

Kunstmuseum Basel

For art aficionados, the Kunstmuseum Basel is a hidden gem, featuring one of Europe's oldest and most significant public art collections. The museum features paintings from the Middle Ages to the present, including works by Holbein, Picasso, and contemporary artists.

Tinguely Fountain (Tinguely-Brunnen).

Swiss artist Jean Tinguely designed this fanciful fountain, which is a humorous contemporary art piece in the middle of the city. Its mechanical sculptures shower water in unexpected ways, captivating people of all ages.

Strasbourg, France

SCAN THE QR CODE

1. Open your device's camera app.
2. Align the QR code within the camera frame.
3. Wait for the code to be recognized.
4. Check the displayed notification or link.
5. Tap to access the linked content or information.

~ 39 ~

Rhine River Promenade

Take a leisurely walk along the Rhine River Promenade, where you may enjoy river views, relax at riverfront cafés, or board one of the classic Rhine ferries.

Beyeler Foundation (Fondation Beyeler)

This famous art museum, located just outside of the city, has a private collection of modern and contemporary art in a gorgeous Renzo Piano-designed edifice. It's worth the short drive for its remarkable collection and serene surroundings.

How To Get To Basel

By Air

The nearest airport, EuroAirport Basel-Mulhouse-Freiburg (BSL), serves both Switzerland and France. It is approximately 5 kilometres from the city centre. From the airport, you can take a bus or taxi to the city.

• Bus: The No. 50 bus takes about 15 minutes from the airport to Basel's main train station, with tickets costing around CHF 5-7.

By train

Basel is a major rail hub with excellent connections throughout Europe.

• From Zurich: Trains are frequent and take about an hour, with ticket prices ranging from CHF 20-40.

• From Paris: The high-speed TGV train takes approximately three hours and costs between €50 and €100.

• From Frankfurt: The train journey takes approximately 2.5 hours and costs between €40 and €80.

by car

Basel is easily accessible by car from major European cities, with excellent connections to Zurich, Freiburg, and Strasbourg. The city provides numerous parking options, though they can be expensive.

Cost of exploring Basel

• **Accommodation**

• Budget: CHF 80-120 per night.

• Mid-range: CHF 150 to 200 per night

• Luxury: CHF 250+ per night

• **Dining:**

- Budget meal: CHF 15-25
- Mid-range restaurant: CHF 40-60 per person
- Fine dining: CHF 80+ per person
- **transport:**
- Local tram or bus ticket: CHF 3.80
- Rhine ferry: CHF 2-5 (depending on the route)
- **Attraction:**
- Basel Minster: Free (small fee for tower climb)
- Kunstmuseum Basel: CHF 26
- Beyeler Foundation: CHF 25

Chapter 5. Discover Hidden Gems and Quaint Villages

St. Goar and Lorelei Rock

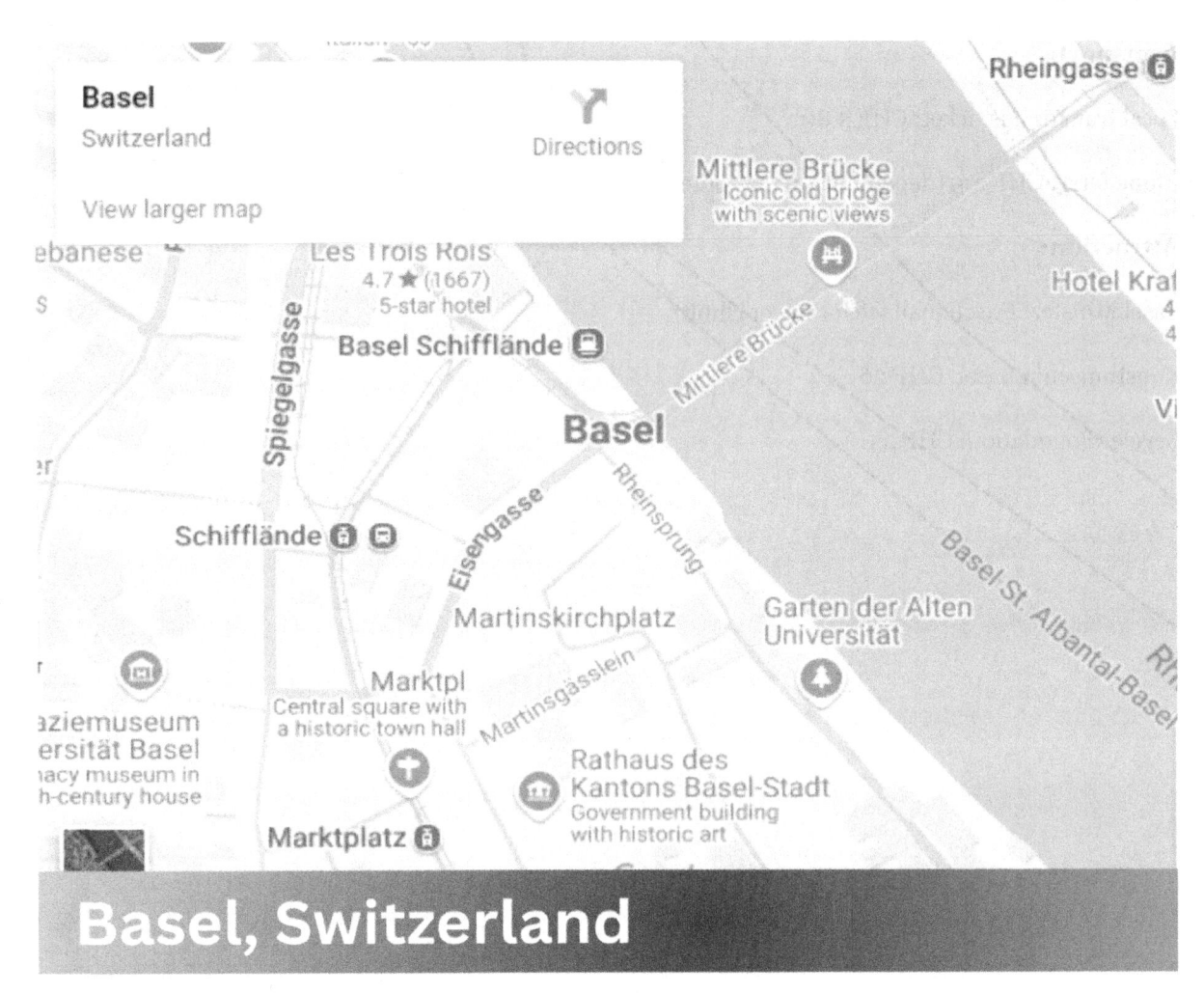

Basel, Switzerland

SCAN THE QR CODE

1. Open your device's camera app.
2. Align the QR code within the camera frame.
3. Wait for the code to be recognized.
4. Check the displayed notification or link.
5. Tap to access the linked content or information.

St. Goar, a lovely village on the Middle Rhine, is known for its closeness to the iconic Lorelei Rock. This sheer slate cliff stands 132 meters above the river and has inspired legends about a siren tempting sailors to their demise with her voice. Visitors may take a short walk or boat journey from town to the Lorelei Rock, which offers stunning views of the Rhine Gorge, a UNESCO World Heritage site. St. Goar is famous for the spectacular Rheinfels Castle, which provides insight into the region's mediaeval past.

How to Get There

By train

St Goar is served by regional trains on the Koblenz-Mainz line.

• From Koblenz: The train takes around 30 minutes and costs roughly €8-€12.

• Trains departing from Frankfurt take around 1.5 hours and cost €20.

By boat

Cruises along the Rhine often stop at St. Goar, providing travellers with a picturesque view of the river and the Lorelei Rock.

Cost

• Hiking the Lorelei Rock is free (open to the public).

• Boat tours to Lorelei Rock cost €10-€15.

Bacharach • A Fairytale Village

Breisach: The Gateway to the Black Forest.

Breisach, located on the banks of the Rhine River, is frequently regarded as the entrance to Germany's lovely Black Forest area. This lovely town has a blend of mediaeval and contemporary beauty, with landmarks such as the St. Stephen's Cathedral (Breisacher Münster) provides panoramic views of the Rhine and adjacent vineyards. Breisach is also a popular starting place for exploring the Black Forest's deep forests, quaint towns, and picturesque hiking paths.

How to Get There

By train

Breisach is readily accessible from Freiburg by regional rail.

• From Freiburg: The train takes roughly 30 minutes and costs between €7 and €10.

by car

Breisach is about a 30-minute drive from Freiburg along the B31 route. Parking is provided throughout the town.

Cost

• St. Stephen's Cathedral is free to see.

• Guided Black Forest trips from Breisach: €30 to €50 per person (depending on the itinerary).

Chapter 6. Onboard Activities and Entertainment

Local Wine and Cuisine Tastings

One of the delights of a Rhine River cruise is the ability to sample the region's renowned wine and food without ever leaving the ship. Many river cruise companies provide guided wine tastings and gourmet dining experiences that highlight the unique flavours of the areas they visit. These onboard activities will immerse you in the culinary traditions of the Rheingau, Moselle, and Alsace areas, which are known for their superb white wines, such as Riesling, and hearty local cuisine.

Wine Tasting

Onboard wine tastings sometimes include choices from local vineyards along the Rhine, enabling you to try various varieties from the comfort of the ship. Expert sommeliers lead these sessions, describing the history, characteristics, and tasting notes of the wines, which usually include Riesling, Pinot Gris, Gewürztraminer, and local Pinot Noirs. Some cruises even bring local winemakers on board to exhibit their wines and give insights into their production methods.

Cuisine Tastings

Regional specialities are often included on Rhine River boat menus. Guests may expect to eat delicacies like these:

- Rheingauer Spundekäs is a creamy cheese spread served with fresh bread and local Riesling.

- Sauerbraten: A German pot roast accompanied with dumplings and red cabbage.

- Flammekueche (Tarte Flambée): Alsace's thin, crispy flatbread topped with crème fraîche, onions, and bacon.

- Black Forest Cake: A rich delicacy constructed with layers of chocolate cake, whipped cream, and cherries marinated in kirsch.

Some cruises include participatory culinary activities like as cooking demos, in which chefs demonstrate how to produce regional specialities.

Cost of onboard tastings

- Wine Tastings: Many river cruises offer wine tastings as part of the overall package; however, premium or exclusive wine-tasting sessions may be charged extra. Prices for unique wine tastings vary from €20 and €50 per person, depending on the selection and the presence of skilled sommeliers or winemakers.

- Cuisine Tastings: Onboard meals are often included in the cruise ticket, with speciality dining experiences or cookery workshops available for an additional fee of €30-€70 per person, depending on the menu and exclusivity.

Enhanced Experiences

Some cruise companies provide food and wine-focused shore excursions, such as visits to local vineyards, tastings at a winemaker's estate, and dining at Michelin-starred restaurants. These beach excursions normally cost between €50-€150 per person.

Cultural Performances and Lectures

A Rhine River cruise gives more than simply breathtaking scenery and historical sites; it also provides a thorough exploration of the region's rich cultural legacy via onboard performances and expert-led talks. These activities are intended to broaden your awareness of the places you visit by providing insights into local customs, history, and the arts.

Cultural performances

Many cruise companies provide live performances reflecting the different cultural influences of the Rhine River area. These performances may include:

• Classical Music Concerts: Because the Rhine is close to places with great musical traditions, such as Cologne and Strasbourg, it is customary to attend aboard concerts showcasing the works of composers like Beethoven, Bach, and Mozart. These concerts might be by local musicians or professional bands.

• Traditional Folklore Shows: Some cruise lines provide folk performances that highlight regional music and dance, such as Rhenish or Alsatian folk dances. These vibrant performances often include traditional costumes, instruments, and singing, providing a glimpse of the region's cultural traditions.

• Wine and Song Evenings: A relaxed and engaging event where you may taste local wines while listening to live music celebrating Rhine vineyard traditions. These parties often involve accordion or string performances, creating a welcoming, community environment.

Lectures and Talks

In addition to entertainment, most river excursions have onboard lectures and seminars given by local specialists, historians, and guides. These seminars cover a broad variety of subjects pertinent to the Rhine River and the sites along its route, including:

• History of the Rhine: Discover the Rhine's historical importance as a crucial trading route, its role in European politics, and the stories surrounding its castles and towns, like the Lorelei Rock.

• Art and Architecture: Some lectures highlight the renowned Gothic cathedrals, castles, and mediaeval villages you'll see along the Rhine, such as the famed Cologne Cathedral and Heidelberg Castle.

• Wine and Gastronomy: Experts provide insights into the Rhine Valley's winemaking traditions, namely the creation of Riesling, as well as the region's gastronomic legacy. These discussions may be combined with tastings to provide an immersive experience.

Cost for Cultural Performances and Lectures

• acts: Most cultural acts, such as live music or folk shows, are usually included in the total cost of the trip. Special performances or exclusive events may need an extra cost ranging from €20-€50 per participant.

• Lectures: Onboard lectures and educational discussions are often included in the cruise package, offering an additional chance to learn more about the Rhine and its cultural past.

Chapter 7. Must-See Landmarks along the Rhine

Rhine castles and mediaeval ruins

One of the most memorable parts of a Rhine River cruise is the ability to see the countless castles and mediaeval ruins that dot the landscape along the riverbanks. These fortifications, positioned on high slopes, provide a window into the region's turbulent history of feudal lords, knights, and strategic warfare. Each castle has a distinct history, from its building in the Middle Ages to its significance in regional power conflicts, commerce, and defence.

A Romantic Journey Along the Middle Rhine

The Middle Rhine Valley, often known as the Romantic Rhine, is the most castle-rich portion of the river. This UNESCO World Heritage Site has approximately 40 castles and strongholds, many of which have been saved or repaired, while others lie in haunting ruins. As your boat travels through this gorgeous area, you will see historic fortresses rising over the river, surrounded by luscious vineyards and picturesque cities.

Notable Rhine Castles and Ruins

Marksburg Castle (Braubach): The only castle on the Rhine that has never been destroyed, Marksburg Castle is an excellent example of a well-preserved mediaeval stronghold. Built in the 12th century, it provides tourists with a genuine experience with its historic defences, towers, and interiors. A guided tour will take you into the castle's armoury, great hall, and spectacular battlements.

- Entry Fee: around €10-€15 per person.

Rheinstein Castle (Trechtingshausen): This 14th-century fortification, perched spectacularly on a rock above the river, has been expertly rebuilt. It is recognised for its breathtaking vistas, spectacular Gothic architecture, and a drawbridge that is still operational today. Rheinstein is especially romantic, providing excursions and even weddings in its idyllic location.

- Entry Fee: around €7-€10 per person.

Burg Katz and Burg Maus (St. Goarshausen): These two neighbouring castles, named after a cat and a mouse, confront each other on opposing banks of the river. Though Burg Katz is not available to the public, Burg Maus often conducts falconry exhibitions, making it a family-friendly destination with a long history of mediaeval rivalry.

- Entry Fee: Adults usually pay between €6 and €8 to enter Burg Maus.

Rheinfels Castle (St. Goar): Once the biggest stronghold on the Rhine, Rheinfels Castle is now a fascinating ruin where tourists may explore its wide gardens and underground passages. It was built in the 13th century and had an important function in guarding the area from invaders and collecting taxes on passing ships. Today, the castle contains a museum dedicated to the history of the Rhine and the life of the people who formerly occupied these strongholds.

- Entry Fee: Approximately €5-7 per person.

Pfalzgrafenstein Castle (Kaub): Known for its peculiar position on a tiny island in the middle of the Rhine, Pfalzgrafenstein was formerly a toll castle that regulated river trade in the 14th century. Visitors may take a boat to the island and visit the well-preserved interior of this castle, which was crucial to the region's economy throughout the Middle Ages.

• Entry Fee: Around €5-€6 per person (plus boat costs).

Mediaeval ruins

While many of the Rhine's castles have been repaired, some others remain in ruins, their decaying walls and towers serving as a frightening reminder of times gone. These ruins, which are often surrounded by nature, provide a mysterious quality to the Rhine's scenery.

• Ehrenfels Castle: A 13th-century ruin near Rüdesheim, Ehrenfels was once a strong toll-collecting castle. Despite being in ruins today, its stunning position and history make it a popular tourist destination for those interested in the mediaeval past.

• Reichenstein Castle: Previously a ruin, Reichenstein has been partly restored and now offers tourists a combination of surviving mediaeval buildings and interesting remains to explore.

Cost and accessibility

The majority of the Rhine castles are accessible via guided tours or private investigation. Many river cruise trips include visits to these castles on their itinerary, although many may also be reached by local railroads, boats, or riverside walking paths.

• Entry Fees: Prices vary based on the castle, but normally range between €5 and €15 per person. Some, such as Marksburg and Rheinstein, provide cheap admission to children and families.

• How to Get There: Many castles are readily accessible from important Rhine towns like Koblenz, Bingen, and St. Goar by foot, boat, or bus. Some cruise companies also offer specialised shore excursions centred on castle visits, which often include transportation and guided tours.

UNESCO World Heritage Sites

St. Mary's Cathedral and St. Michael's Church in Hildesheim, Germany

St. Mary's Cathedral and St. Michael's Church, both in the ancient town of Hildesheim, are among Europe's greatest examples of Ottonian Romanesque architecture. Both buildings are UNESCO World Heritage Sites, known for their distinct architectural style, historical importance, and exceptional art.

St. Mary's Cathedral (Hildesheim Cathedral).

St. Mary's Cathedral (also known as Hildesheim Cathedral) is one of Germany's most spectacular Romanesque buildings, dating from the 11th to 12th century. The cathedral's simplicity, with its bold, rounded arches and enormous columns, is typical of Ottonian architecture. Inside, you'll discover treasures like as the Bernward Doors, which show biblical events in exquisite bronze reliefs, and the Christus Column, a gigantic masterpiece that tells the story of Christ. The Thousand-Year-Old Rosebush, which is thought to be over a millennium old, grows on the cathedral's walls as well, symbolising Hildesheim's faith's persistence.

Saint Michael's Church

St. Michael's Church, erected at the same time, is a prime example of early Romanesque architecture, with its symmetrical, geometric design representing the order of divine creation. Inside, the church is home to the painted wooden ceiling, an astonishing picture of Christ's genealogy that spans the whole nave. The bright paintings, columns, and majestic altar are features that represent the period's spiritual and artistic traditions.

Cost

• Entry to the Cathedral and Museum costs around €6 for adults and €4 for students and seniors. Children under 14 may enter for free.

• St. Michael's Church: Admission to the church is usually free, however contributions are accepted for upkeep.

• Guided Tours are available for an extra price of €3-€5 per participant.

City of Strasbourg • Grande Île and Neustadt, France

Strasbourg, the capital of the Alsace region in northern France, has two UNESCO World Heritage Sites: Grande Île and Neustadt. Grande Île is Strasbourg's historic core, known for its timber-framed homes, meandering lanes, and iconic structures like the Cathedral of Notre-Dame, which looms magnificently above the plaza. In contrast, Neustadt recalls Strasbourg's 19th-century growth, with wide boulevards and German-influenced architecture.

What to Explore:

Grande île:

• Cathedral of Notre Dame: This Gothic masterpiece has beautiful stained glass and an astronomical clock.

• Petite France: A beautiful region with waterways and attractive houses, ideal for strolls.

• Maison Kammerzell: A stunningly maintained 15th-century mansion noted for its elaborate façade and dining choices.

Neustadt:

• Palais Universitaire: An impressive neo-Renaissance structure that houses a university and an art museum.

• Place de la République: An exquisite plaza surrounded by significant governmental and cultural facilities; ideal for taking in the ambience.

• Parc de l'Étoile: A wonderful park perfect for a tranquil escape from the city bustle.

Cost:

• Admission to the Cathedral is free, however, the tower visit costs a little charge (about €5).

- Museum admission charges range from €5 to €15, with free admittance on the first Sunday of each month.

- Restaurant choices vary from modest cafés to sophisticated restaurants, with meals ranging between €15 and €30.

Zollverein Coal Mine Industrial Complex (Essen, Germany)

The Zollverein Coal Mine Industrial Complex, in Essen, Germany, is a UNESCO World Legacy Site known for its distinctive Bauhaus architecture and extensive industrial legacy. It was formerly one of the world's biggest and most advanced coal mines, but it has since been turned into a thriving cultural and creative powerhouse.

What to Explore:

Mining Museum: Through interactive exhibits and displays, visitors may learn about coal mining history and its influence on the area.

Architecture Tours: Discover the amazing industrial architecture, such as the landmark Shaft 12 and the Zollverein School of Management and Design.

Cultural Events: Attend exhibits, concerts, and festivals hosted throughout the year in the complex's venues.

Café & Restaurants: Enjoy local food and drinks at the on-site restaurants, which often provide a combination of traditional and modern cuisines.

Walking Paths: Take a stroll around the beautifully manicured gardens, which include historic industrial buildings and contemporary artworks.

Cost:

Entry to the Zollverein is normally free, however, certain attractions, such as the Mining Museum, may levy a small fee of €5-€10. Guided tours and special exhibits may charge different costs, so check their official website for current rates and special events.

The Palace and Gardens of Augustusburg and Falkenlust (Brühl, Germany)

The Palace and Gardens of Augustusburg and Falkenlust, in Brühl, Germany, are outstanding examples of Baroque architecture and gardening that have been designated as UNESCO World Heritage sites. Augustusburg Palace, constructed in the mid-18th century, includes spectacular interiors with delicate stucco work, lavish furniture, and a grand staircase created by architect Balthasar Neumann. Visitors may tour the beautiful chambers, including the majestic royal room, and see the breathtaking views from the palace balcony.

The surrounding grounds are stunning, with groomed lawns, elegant fountains, and brilliant seasonal flowers in the formal manner of the period. Falkenlust, the quaint hunting lodge, is only a short walk away and provides a more private, yet still excellent, experience with its gorgeous surroundings and decorative components.

Explorations might include strolls around the gardens, guided tours of the palace, and picnics on the grounds. The whole experience depicts the grandeur of the 18th century and the life of Elector Clemens August.

The cost of admission to the palace varies; adults normally pay roughly €10, with reductions available for the elderly and students. Garden entry may be free or included with palace tickets. Open hours and costs ay change according to the season, so check ahead of time.

Scenic Vineyards and Landscapes River Valley

The Mosel River Valley is a breathtakingly beautiful area of Germany, famed for its vineyards, attractive towns, and steep, terraced slopes along the Mosel River. The Mosel River, which flows into the Rhine near Koblenz, is famed for its white wines, particularly Riesling, and provides tourists with stunning vistas interrupted by ancient castles and small villages such as Cochem and Bernkastel-Kues.

Mosel River Valley is readily accessible from large cities like Frankfurt and Cologne. The area is accessible by rail, with services running to places along the Mosel River, such as Traben-Trarbach and Zell. Car rentals are very popular for taking picturesque roads along the river.

Cost: A day excursion might cost between €50 and €100 per person, which includes transport, food and wine tastings at nearby wineries. For a more casual stay, plan to pay between €80 and €150 per night, depending on the sort of accommodation selected.

Rüdesheim am Rhein.

Rüdesheim am Rhein is a lovely village set in Germany's magnificent Rhine Valley, famed for its attractive half-timbered buildings, flourishing vineyards, and breathtaking views along the Rhine. Rüdesheim, is a popular tourist destination, with attractions like the famed Drosselgasse, a busy street lined with wine bars and stores, and the majestic Niederwalddenkmal monument, which overlooks the river and affords panoramic views of the surrounding landscapes.

Cost:

A day trip to Rüdesheim may be rather inexpensive. Train rates from Frankfurt normally vary from €15 to €30 each way, while parking in town costs between €2 and €4 per day. Meals at local restaurants might cost anything from €10 to €25, depending on your preferences. Overall, a budget of €50 to €100 is appropriate for a day trip, depending on activities and food options.

Getting there:

Rüdesheim am Rhein is readily accessible by many kinds of transportation. If you're travelling by rail, there are direct trains from Frankfurt (approximately an hour away) to Rüdesheim station. For those driving, the town is situated on the B42 and is about 45 minutes from Frankfurt. Additionally, river cruises down the Rhine often stop at Rüdesheim, providing a unique viewpoint on the region's splendour.

Lorelei Rock

Lorelei Rock is a picturesque and renowned limestone rock on the Rhine River in Germany, near St. Goarshausen. The rock, which rises around 120 meters above the lake, is famous for its breathtaking vistas and the tales that surround it, notably the myth of Lorelei, a siren who lured sailors to their deaths with her alluring singing.

The area around Lorelei Rock is part of the Rhine Gorge, a UNESCO World Heritage Site famed for its beautiful scenery, castles, and vineyards. Visitors may visit vistas that provide sweeping views of the Rhine and the picturesque towns along its banks.

Lorelei Rock may be reached by rail from major German cities such as Frankfurt or Koblenz. The rock is just a short walk or spectacular boat trip from either town.

Cost to Visit: Visiting Lorelei Rock is free, although boat rides down the Rhine normally cost between €15 and €30 per person, depending on the duration of the voyage. If you choose to explore the region with guided excursions, the cost might range from €20 to €100.

Bingen am Rhein.

Bingen am Rhein is a picturesque town in Germany's Rhineland-Palatinate area, where the Rhine and Nahe rivers meet. This scenic site is famed for its breathtaking views of the Rhine Valley, which has rolling vineyards, old castles, and the surrounding Binger Loch, a tiny valley in the river. Visitors may walk along the picturesque waterfront promenade, explore the mediaeval streets, or see famous buildings like as the Gothic-style St. Augustine's Church and the majestic Klopp Castle.

Cost

While admission to the town is free, tourists should pay for activities like castle tours (usually between €5 and €10) and meals at local restaurants, which may cost from €10 to €25 per person depending on the location. Tickets for a picturesque boat cruise on the Rhine normally cost between €15 and €30.

Getting There

Bingen am Rhein is readily accessible by rail, with frequent connections from Mainz and Frankfurt. The rail ride from Frankfurt takes around 50 minutes. If you prefer to drive, it is about an hour from Frankfurt, and there is plenty of parking in town.

Chapter 8. Excursions and Activities at Every Stop

Guided Walking Tours

Guided walking excursions on a Rhine River cruise provide an engaging approach for travellers to see the Rhine Valley's rich history, culture, and breathtaking beauty. These trips often take you past picturesque towns and villages, old castles, wineries, and breathtaking scenery along one of Europe's most well-known river itineraries.

Highlights of Guided Walking Tour

Cultural Insights: Wander through attractive towns such as Rüdesheim, Bacharach, and Mainz, where local guides tell tales about the region's history, architecture, and wines.

Scenic Views: Many walking trips feature paths along riverbanks or through vineyards, providing spectacular views of the Rhine Valley and its renowned castles set on hilltops.

Local Cuisine: Some trips may include tastings of local specialities, such as Rhine wines and regional cuisine.

Flexible Itineraries: Tours may be of varying lengths and suited to various fitness levels, offering a memorable experience for everyone.

Cost

The cost of guided walking excursions on a Rhine River cruise varies according to the ship operator and tour selections. Half-day trips typically cost between €20 and €50 per person, while full-day excursions may vary from €50 to €100. Many cruise packages offer guided excursions as part of their overall itinerary.

How To Book

Booking a guided walking tour is normally done via the cruise operator you choose for your Rhine River trip. Here are some major cruise companies that offer Rhine itineraries with guided tours:

Viking River Cruises: Offers a range of Rhine itineraries, including free shore excursions.

• Site: [Viking River Cruises](https://www.vikingrivercruises.com).

Avalon Waterways: Offers unusual activities, such as walking tours, that may be booked online.

• Site: [Avalon Waterways](https://www.avalonwaterways.com)

Uniworld Boutique River Cruise Collection offers premium river cruises with a variety of guided activities.

• Website: Uniworld (https://www.uniworld.com).

American Cruise Lines provides extensive itineraries and guided excursions of the Rhine area.

• Site: [American Cruise Lines](https://www.americancruiselines.com).

Bike and Hike Along the Rhine

Biking on the Rhine

The Rhine Cycle Route (Rheinradweg) is one of Germany's most popular cycling routes, spanning 1,230 km from its source in Switzerland to the North Sea. The route is well-marked and relatively flat, making it suitable for cyclists of all abilities. Key attractions of the bike path include:

• Picturesque Villages: Cyclists may stop in attractive towns like Bacharach, Rüdesheim, and Boppard, where half-timbered buildings and local cafés provide a glimpse into regional culture.

• Castles and Fortresses: The famed "Romantic Rhine" is home to various castles, including Marksburg and Burg Katz, built on hilltops overlooking the river, making for fantastic picture possibilities.

• Vineyards and Wine Tours: The German Rhine area is well-known for its Riesling wines. Many vineyards provide wine tastings and excursions, enabling bikers to enjoy the local flavours.

Hiking Along The Rhine

For those who enjoy hiking, several routes meander through the Rhine Valley, including portions of the Rheinsteig, a prime hiking route spanning around 320 km. The highlights of trekking along the Rhine are:

• Awesome Views: Hikers will enjoy breathtaking panoramic views of the river, terraced vineyards, and lush wooded slopes.

• Historical Sites: The paths take you to historical monuments like old ruins and abbeys, which provide cultural value to your walk.

• Nature and animals: The regional parks along the Rhine are home to a rich flora and fauna, allowing for animal observation.

Tips

• Best Time to Visit: The best time to bike and walk along the Rhine is from late spring (May) to early fall (September) when the weather is nice and the scenery is beautiful.

• Safety and Gear: Make sure you have the proper gear, such as comfortable clothes, sturdy hiking boots, and, if bike, a helmet. Carry lots of water and food, particularly when travelling to more distant places.

• Plan Your itinerary: Plan your itinerary and make reservations in advance, particularly during high tourist season.

Riverfront Cafés and Local Markets

Riverfront Cafés

Café Blum in Koblenz, Germany

• Location: Near Deutsches Eck (German Corner).

• Description: This ancient café is well-known for its breathtaking views of the Rhine and Moselle river's confluence. Café Blum, first opened in 1825, provides a range of delicacies, including its famous German cakes and classic coffee. Patrons may enjoy their goodies on the terrace, which overlooks the river.

Rheincafé (in Bonn, Germany)

• Location: Friedrichstraße, Bonn.

• Description: Rheincafé, located right on the Rhine River, provides a relaxing ambience with outdoor seating and panoramic views of the river and the opposite side. It's the ideal area to relax with a drink or a little lunch, particularly during the warmer months.

Café de Flore, Strasbourg, France

• Location: Quai des Bateliers, Strasbourg.

• Description: This café, nestled amid the gorgeous canals flowing into the Rhine, emanates a charm that reflects Strasbourg's creative flair. It is well-known for its native Alsatian cuisine and outstanding coffee, and it is a great place to eat while watching boats pass by.

Riverside Café (in Cologne, Germany)

• Location: Schildergasse, close to Rheinauhafen area

• Description: This modern café has a breathtaking view of Cologne Cathedral and the Rhine River. It offers both indoor and outdoor seating, making it a comfortable place to enjoy freshly made coffee, pastries, and light meals.

Local Markets

Marktplatz, Koblenz, Germany

• Location: central Koblenz, a short walk from the Rhine.

• Description: This busy area is home to a colourful market with local sellers selling fresh vegetables, speciality delicacies, and handcrafted crafts. It's a great place for travellers to try local cuisine and pick up unusual gifts.

Bonn Market (Bonn, Germany).

• Location: Münsterplatz, near Bonn University.

• Description: This weekly market offers a variety of vendors selling fresh fruits, vegetables, cheeses, and flowers. The lovely setting against the background of the Bonn Minster adds to the market's allure.

Christmas Market in Strasbourg, France.

Location: Place Broglie, Strasbourg.

• Description: One of Europe's most renowned Christmas markets, this market offers handmade decorations, local specialities like gingerbread and mulled wine, and a joyful ambience. The market runs from late November to late December and provides a magnificent experience along the Rhine.

Ludwigshafen Market (Ludwigshafen, Germany).

• Location: Wilhelmstraße, along the Rhine

• Description: This bustling market has a diverse range of vendors selling everything from fresh fruit to baked items. It's an excellent chance to get to know the locals while also trying traditional German cuisine.

Chapter 9. Practical Tips for a Smooth Cruise.

Understanding Local Culture and Etiquette.

Regional Overview

Switzerland: Known for its breathtaking scenery and neutrality, Swiss culture is a fusion of German, French, and Italian elements. Communication is essential; although German is prominent in the north, French is spoken in the west. The Swiss emphasise timeliness and efficiency, therefore it is customary to welcome with a strong handshake. Furthermore, tipping is usual at restaurants, but the service fee is often included in the bill.

France (Alsace area): The Alsace area, situated on the Rhine's northeastern banks, is a rich fusion of French and German traditions. Here, you will discover distinct traditions ranging from wine-tasting etiquette to the significance of local festivities like Christmas markets. A simple "Bonjour" upon entering a store and "Merci, au revoir" when leaving is welcomed. Dining is an important element of culture; meals are frequently lengthy, and it is considered impolite to hurry.

Germany (Rhineland): The Rhineland is known for its lively festivals, especially the Cologne Carnival. Germans often respect directness and dependability. Unless specifically requested differently, greetings are normally formal, including titles and last names. Punctuality is expected in both corporate and social settings. Wait for the host to begin before eating, and if you are asked to someone's house, bringing a modest gift, such as flowers or wine, is a kind gesture.

The Dutch culture along the Rhine emphasises egalitarian principles and directness. The expression "doe maar normal" (simply act normal) captures this mindset. When meeting someone, a solid handshake is expected. The Dutch are noted for their hospitality, and when welcomed to a Dutch house, it is customary to send a modest gift. Dining customs include keeping elbows off the table and eating only after everyone has been served.

Local Customs and Etiquette

Communication Style: Across the Rhine, communication differs. The Swiss and Germans often favour direct communication, while the French and Dutch may use more subtle or indirect ways. Context is important—a deep understanding of cultural variances may improve relationships.

Dining Etiquette: Dining traditions might differ widely. In parts of Northern Europe, including the Netherlands and Germany, completing your dish is considered courteous and a compliment to the cook. In contrast, in France, leaving a tiny sum is often accepted.

Public Behaviour: In most Rhine areas, public behaviour is governed by a sense of propriety. It is important to speak at a fair volume and avoid encroaching on others' personal space. Personal space and tranquillity on public transit are widely respected, especially in Switzerland and Germany.

Festivals & Celebrations: Attending local festivals is a great way to connect with the culture. Understanding the importance of these events heightens enjoyment. For example, the Rhine in Flames event, noted for its pyrotechnics and lit boats, is a magnificent celebration in Germany that emphasises community solidarity.

Transportation

Getting There

Train

Common Routes to the Rhine River

From Frankfurt to Cologne.

- Duration: Around an hour.
- Train: Intercity Express (ICE).
- Departure Terminal: Frankfurt Hauptbahnhof (Main Station).
- Arrival Terminal: Köln Hauptbahnhof (Cologne's main station).
- Cost: Between €30 and €50 for a one-way ticket, depending on how long in advance you book.

From Amsterdam to Düsseldorf.

- Duration: Around 2.5 hours.
- Train: intercity or high-speed ICR trains.
- The departure terminal is Amsterdam Centraal.
- Arrival Terminal: Düsseldorf Hauptbahnhof.
- Cost: One-way tickets range between €30 and €45.

From Zurich to Basel

- Duration: Around an hour.
- Train: Intercity (IC) trains.
- The departure terminal is Zurich Hauptbahnhof.
- Arrival Terminal: Basel-SBB.

• Cost: Around CHF 25 to CHF 40 for a one-way ticket.

From Paris to Strasbourg.

• Duration: Around two hours.

• Train: TGV (Train de Grande Vitesse).

• Departure Terminal: Paris, Gare de l'Est.

• Arrival Terminal: Strasbourg Gare.

• Cost: A one-way ticket typically costs between €35 and €70.

Key Train Terminals along the Rhine

• Koln Hauptbahnhof (Cologne): A significant hub that connects to other European locations and is an excellent starting point for exploring the Rhine River. The station lies in the middle of the city, among sights such as the Cologne Cathedral.

• Mainz Hauptbahnhof: Serves as a gateway to the Rhine Valley, with scenic towns such as Rüdesheim and Bingen close by. It links with regional trains and provides service to bigger cities.

• Bonn Hauptbahnhof: Another ancient city along the Rhine, Bonn's station offers easy access to river cruises and attractions.

• Basel SBB: Basel is a key station serving the tri-national region of France, Germany, and Switzerland, and it acts as an essential hub for Rhine traffic.

Booking & Discounts

• Tickets are often available for purchase online in advance via railway company websites or at train station kiosks. It is essential to look for special reduced rates, particularly on regional trains or when booking circular journeys.

• Eurail Pass and Interrail Pass: If you want to travel extensively around Europe, these passes provide flexibility and may save money, particularly on numerous visits.

Car

Cars and Routes

Popular Starting Points: If you're coming from a large city like Zurich (Switzerland), Frankfurt (Germany), or Amsterdam (Netherlands), you have a few choices.

From Zurich, Switzerland:

• Route: Take the A1 highway to Winterthur, then connect the A5 to reach the Rhine near Basel.

• Distance: Approximately 85 km (53 miles), a one-hour trip.

From Frankfurt, Germany:

• Route: Head west on the A66, then take the A60 towards Mainz and connect to the B9 along the Rhine.

• Distance: Approximately 80 km (50 miles), or a one-hour trip.

From Amsterdam, the Netherlands:

• Route: Take the A2 to Utrecht, then the A12 to Arnhem to connect with the Rhine.

• Distance: Approximately 100 km (62 miles), or a 1.5-hour trip.

Terminals and Access Points

Accessing the Rhine River is simple, with various terminals and ports catering to both tourists and freight. Key terminals include:

• Basel Mulhouse Airport (Switzerland): An important entrance point, situated around 10 km from the Rhine. Car rentals are available.

• Mainz: Known for its attractive old town and as a gateway to the Rhine, ideal for visitors looking to enjoy the river's stunning sights.

• Cologne: Provides complete river cruise facilities, as well as convenient access to the A4 and A57 highways.

Costs

When planning a journey to the Rhine by vehicle, consider the following expenses:

Fuel Costs:

• As of October 2023, average gasoline costs in Europe are approximately €1.50 per litre ($6.00 per gallon). A drive from Frankfurt to Mainz (80 km) may need 5-6 litres (1.3 to 1.6 gallons), costing between €7.50-€9.00 ($8.50-$10.25).

Toll and Fees:

Depending on your route, tolls may apply. For example, driving on certain Swiss roads needs a vignette, which costs about CHF 40 (roughly €38 or $42) each year.

Parking:

- Cities along the Rhine often have paid parking, which costs between €2-€3 per hour (€20-€30 for the whole day).

Car Rental:

- Daily automobile rental fees might vary from €30 and €80, depending on the vehicle type and rental operator.

Boat/Cruise

The Rhine River, one of Europe's longest and most important rivers, passes through four countries: Switzerland, France, Germany, and the Netherlands. Travelling down the Rhine by boat or cruise provides a unique opportunity to see the stunning scenery, fascinating cities, and rich history that line its banks. This is a guide to the itineraries, terminals, and expenses related to Rhine river cruises.

Popular routes

Amsterdam to Basel:

- This extensive route passes through some of the most beautiful areas of the Rhine. Starting in Amsterdam, you will journey south via gorgeous places such as Düsseldorf, Cologne, and Koblenz before arriving in Basel, Switzerland.

- Highlights include a cruise along the Rhine Gorge, a UNESCO World Heritage Site known for its castles and vineyards.

Koblenz to Strasbourg:

- This route focuses on the Rhine's German and French parts. You'll leave Koblenz and explore places like Rüdesheim and Mannheim before crossing into France and ending in Strasbourg.

- The Rhine Valley is well-known for its wine production, notably Riesling, and provides several options for vineyard excursions and tastings.

Cologne to Amsterdam:

- A shorter trip that enables travellers to see the exciting metropolis of Cologne as well as the picturesque splendour of the Dutch countryside. Bonn and Düsseldorf may be among the stops along the trip.

- This itinerary is great for individuals seeking a brief holiday while seeing important cultural sites.

Rhine In Flames:

- Special seasonal excursions are available throughout the summer months when several cities along the Rhine host fireworks displays. These excursions often take place on weekends and provide a unique nighttime experience along the river.

Terminals and Port

- Amsterdam Passenger Terminal: Conveniently located in the city centre, this terminal serves as a hub for several cruise lines and offers convenient access to the city's attractions.

- Cologne Cruise Terminal: Close to the city, making it ideal for sightseeing. The terminal has good facilities and transportation options.

- Koblenz Cruise port: This port, situated near the junction of the Moselle and Rhine rivers, offers access to a variety of cruise routes.

- Basel EuroAirport and Rhine Port: Basel has links to both a river cruise terminal and an airport, making it a convenient beginning or finishing location for your voyage.

- Strasbourg Port: Conveniently placed in the city centre, this port allows tourists to see the lovely city of Strasbourg, which combines French and German culture.

Costs

Rhine River cruise prices vary greatly based on several parameters, including trip length, season, and kind of hotel. Here's a broad outline of the charges you should expect:

- Short Cruises (3-5 Days): These cruises normally cost $500 to $1,200 per person and include meals and some activities.

- Long Cruises (7-10 days): Prices vary from $1,200 to $3,500 per person, depending on cabin type and amenities. Some premium lines may charge up to $4,000 for suites or all-inclusive packages.

- Luxurious Cruises: High-end cruise lines often charge $5,000 to $10,000 or more for luxurious rooms, gourmet cuisine, and exclusive shore excursions.

- Extra Costs: While meals are often included, travellers should plan for excursions, beverages, gratuities, and any extra activities not included in the cruise package.

Flights (to adjacent airports)

Nearby Airports

Frankfurt Airport (FRA) in Germany

- Distance to Rhine River: About 30 kilometres (18 miles) to Mainz and Wiesbaden.

- Airlines: Major international carriers include Lufthansa, United Airlines, Air France, and others.

Cologne Bonn Airport (CGN) in Germany

- Distance to the Rhine River: Cologne, one of the Rhine's greatest cities, is about 60 kilometres (37 miles) away.

• Airlines: Ryanair and Eurowings are low-cost carriers, as are established airlines.

Basel-Mulhouse Airport (BSL/MLH/EAP) in Switzerland/France

• Distance to Rhine River: About 80 kilometres (50 miles) to the Rhine River banks at Basel.

• Airlines include EasyJet, Air France, and others.

Strasbourg Airport (SXB) in France

• Distance to Rhine River: The Rhine in Strasbourg is about 100 kilometres (62 miles) away.

• Airlines include Air France, Lufthansa, and several regional carriers.

Routes and Terminals

• Frankfurt Airport (FRA):

• Terminals include Terminal 1 and Terminal 2. Lufthansa and its partners mostly utilise Terminal 1.

• Connects to Several international flights departing from key cities worldwide.

• Transport Options: Easy access to rail stations that link to Rhine River cities.

• **Cologne Bonn Airport (CGN):**

• Terminal 1 has all amenities centralised.

 • Connects to Mostly European destinations and budget routes.

• Transport Options: Cities along the river may be reached by shuttle buses or rental cars.

• **The Basel-Mulhouse Airport (BSL):**

• Terminals: A single integrated terminal serves all airlines.

• Connects to A variety of inexpensive and established airlines, especially on European routes.

• Transport Options: Regular bus service to Basel and surrounding cities.

• **Airport: Strasbourg (SXB)**

• There is one terminal.

• Connects to: Regional and some international destinations.

• Transport Options: Tram and bus services are available to the city centre and other regions of Strasbourg.

Estimated costs

• Flight costs:

• Economy Class: Depending on the departure city, round-trip ticket rates to Frankfurt may vary from $600 to $1200, while flights to cheap destinations like Cologne Bonn can start as low as $200 to $400 for eurozone travel.

• Low-cost Airlines: If travelling inside Europe, look into cheap airlines that offer flights around $100 if booked in advance.

• Transport costs:

• Train to the Rhine: Trains from Frankfurt to Mainz or Wiesbaden cost between €5 and €15 ($6 and $18) one way and take 30 minutes to an hour.

• Car Rentals: Expect to spend between $30 and $70 per day, depending on season and car type, plus gasoline charges.

• Airport Transfer: Shuttle or taxi services from the airport to Rhine cities might cost between €30 and €100 ($36 and $120), depending on distance and time of day.

Getting Around

River cruises

Popular routes

Amsterdam to Basel:

• Duration: Around 7-8 nights.

• Highlights: Amsterdam's canals, Kinderdijk windmills, Cologne Cathedral, Bonn, Deutsche Eck in Koblenz, Rüdesheim, and the picturesque Rhine Gorge with its spectacular castles.

Basel to Amsterdam:

• Duration: 7–8 nights

• Highlights: The reverse route, which provides vistas of the Black Forest, charming cities such as Strasbourg and Heidelberg, and the Rhine Valley.

Rotterdam to Mainz:

• Duration: Around 8-10 nights.

• Highlights: Rotterdam's contemporary architecture, the Rhine's rich history in places such as Düsseldorf, and Mainz, home to the Gutenberg Museum.

Frankfurt to Cologne:

- Duration: 5–6 nights

- Highlights: Discover urban cultural centres, the lovely village of Rüdesheim, the Lorelei rock, and the dynamic metropolis of Cologne.

Major Terminals

Amsterdam:

- Terminal: Passenger Terminal Amsterdam (PTA).

- Facilities: Conveniently located in the city centre, restaurants, and shopping, with easy access to public transit.

Basel:

- Terminal: Basel Cruise Terminal

- Features: Modern facilities, tourist services, and closeness to the city's historical monuments.

Cologne:

- Terminal: Cologne Bonn Airport (CGN) is quite nearby, and the cruise terminal is situated along the Rhine.

- Features: Local public transportation, tourist information, and neighbouring attractions.

Rhine Gorge:

- Spot: Many cruises will pass via this UNESCO World Heritage site, providing views of the lovely Lorelei rock and the many castles dotting the slopes.

Rüdesheim:

- Terminal: Rüdesheim Cruise Terminal

- Facilities: Wine tasting, cable car access to the Niederwald Monument, and small stores.

Estimated costs

River cruise rates vary greatly depending on the cruise operator, length, season, and cabin class. On average:

- Economy Cruise:

- The cost of a 7-night cruise ranges from €1,000 to €2,500 per person.

- Premium Cruise:

- A 7-night cruise typically costs between €2,500 and €5,000 per person, which includes shore excursions, gourmet cuisine, and free drinks.

- Luxury Cruise:

- Cost: €5,000 to €10,000+ per person for luxury experiences that may include all-inclusive facilities, personalised services, and unique excursions.

Note: Additional charges may apply for shore excursions, onboard gratuities, and optional activities. Early booking or last-minute bargains may result in savings.

Biking

Bike Routes Along the Rhine River

Rhine Cycling Route (EuroVelo 15):

- The Rhine Cycle Route, part of the EuroVelo network, is one of Europe's most well-known bike routes. It follows the river from the Swiss border to the North Sea, passing through numerous countries such as Germany and the Netherlands.

- The route is well-marked and largely follows designated bike lanes, calm roads, and trails. Cyclists may enjoy magnificent vistas of vineyards, castles, and small towns.

Major Routes:

- Basel to Mainz (about 520 kilometres / 323 miles) • This part passes through lovely towns like Breisach, Strasbourg, and Rüdesheim. The terrain is largely flat, making it suitable for cyclists of all skill levels.

- Mainz to Koblenz (about 100 km / 62 miles) • This section of the road is surrounded by vineyards and provides breathtaking views of the Lorelei rock and the majestic Rhine Gorge.

- Koblenz to Cologne (about 150 km / 93 miles) • This portion is notable for its historical importance, with sites like the Ehrenbreitstein Fortress and the city of Bonn.

Local detours and additional routes:

- Many Rhine towns have local cycling lanes that connect to neighbouring attractions including castles, parks, and cultural institutions. Be sure to look at opportunities around Bingen, Rüdesheim, and beyond.

Bike Terminals and Rental Services

Most Rhine River villages provide bike rental and return stations. Here are some highlighted options:

- Köln (Cologne): Shops such as "Köln-Rad" hire bikes and provide guided trips.

- Bonn: Bike rentals are offered at Bonn's major rail station and specialised bike stores.

- Mainz: Several rental firms around the city's historic centre provide easy bike pickup and drop-off locations.

- Rüdesheim: This tourist destination includes many bike rental booths along the shore.

Cost of Biking

The cost of riding along the Rhine varies depending on a number of variables, including bike rental rates, route duration, and hotels.

Bicycle Rentals:

- Standard bike rentals typically cost between €10 and €20 per day. E-bikes are normally priced between €25 and €50 per day.

- If you intend on renting for a few days, several rental companies offer multi-day discounts.

Accommodations:

- Budget accommodations such as hostels and campsites start at about €20-€30 per night. Mid-range hotels may cost between €70 and €150, depending on their location and facilities.

- Consider making reservations in advance, particularly in major tourist destinations.

Food and Drink:

- Meals may be modest (€8-€15 for informal eating) or more sophisticated (€20 and above).

- Don't forget to try local wines, particularly in vineyard areas.

Total Estimated Cost:

- Depending on your tastes and selections, a week-long cycling tour along the Rhine may cost between €500 and €1,000, including bike rental, hotels, food, and incidental charges.

Tips for Biking the Rhine.

- Plan Your Route: Use maps and guidebooks to determine your route and highlight noteworthy sites along the way.

- Stay Hydrated and Prepared: Carry water and food with you when bicycling, particularly on lengthy portions with minimal amenities.

- Be Weather-Ready: The weather might change fast, so bring a light rain jacket and dress in layers.

- Local Etiquette: Respect pedestrian zones and obey local bicycle rules.

Trains

Trains and Routes

Intercity (IC) and Regional (RE) Trains

• Intercity (IC) trains travel longer distances and link important Rhine cities like Cologne (Köln), Düsseldorf, Bonn, Mainz, Wiesbaden, Frankfurt, and Basel.

• Regional (RE) trains service smaller towns along the river and make many stops, making them excellent for visiting particular locations like Rüdesheim, Boppard, and Koblenz.

Typical train routes:

• Cologne to Koblenz: This 1.5-hour route passes through picturesque vineyards and mediaeval cities.

• Koblenz to Mainz: A beautiful journey along the river that takes approximately an hour by regional rail.

• Frankfurt to Bacharach: This gorgeous journey takes around 1 hour and 15 minutes and travels through stunning wine districts.

Scenic Train Rides:

• For a particularly picturesque experience, try using the Rhine Valley line (RB or RE), which connects Koblenz and Bingen. This road is famed for its breathtaking vistas of vineyards, castles, and picturesque towns.

Train terminals

• Cologne Hbf (Hauptbahnhof): The central station is situated directly next to the Cologne Cathedral and acts as a significant hub for trains travelling down the Rhine.

• Koblenz Hbf: Situated at the junction of the Rhine and Moselle rivers, it connects to regional and intercity services.

• Mainz Hbf: Located adjacent to the Rhine, it links travellers to a variety of regional and intercity connections.

• Frankfurt Hbf: One of Germany's busiest rail stations, it serves several domestic and international train lines, making it an excellent starting point for exploring the river.

Costs

• Tickets: Prices vary depending on distance, train type, and prior booking. Here are some estimated prices:

• Cologne to Koblenz: €18-25 for a 1.5-hour travel by IC or RE train.

• Koblenz to Mainz: About €10-15 for a regional rail (RE).

• Frankfurt to Bacharach: Approximately €15-20 for a RE or RB train.

• Discounts: Consider buying a German Rail Pass or a regional day ticket (such as the Rheinland-Pfalz Ticket) for unlimited travel within particular zones, which may be cost-effective if you want to make many excursions in one day. The Rheinland-Pfalz Ticket costs around €27 per person for a party of up to five travellers.

Tips for Travellers

• Plan Ahead: Always check train timetables ahead of time on the official Deutsche Bahn website or app to locate the best connections.

• Seat Reservations: While seat reservations are not required on regional trains, it is sometimes recommended to book seats on intercity trains during busy travel hours, particularly during tourist seasons.

• baggage: Most trains offer enough baggage capacity, but keep a watch on your possessions, particularly at crowded stops.

Ferries

Ferries and Routes

Bingen to Rüdesheim: This is one of the Rhine's most popular ferry routes, linking two picturesque Rhine Gorge villages. The boat voyage provides spectacular vistas of vineyards and mediaeval castles.

Königswinter to Bad Honnef: This ferry route, located near Bonn, spans the Rhine and is well-known for its stunning views of the Siebengebirge mountains, which are particularly lovely in the autumn.

Braubach to Marksburg: This boat is very popular with tourists visiting Marksburg Castle, one of the few Rhine castles that has never been demolished.

Worms to Ingelheim: This route links the old city of Worms with Ingelheim, which is noted for its winemaking culture and lovely surroundings.

Terminals

• Bingen Ferry Terminal: This terminal, located in the centre of Bingen, gives quick access to the Bingen-Rüdesheim ferry service and includes services such as parking and local eateries.

• Rüdesheim Ferry Terminal: Located in the old town, the Rüdesheim terminal provides convenient access to the picturesque streets and vine-covered slopes.

• Königswinter Ferry Terminal: This terminal, located near the town's train station, is ideal for those coming by rail.

• Bad Honnef Ferry port: This port is easily accessible, near to local facilities, and provides stunning views from the coast.

Cost

Ferry rates vary depending on the route, time of year, and if you bring a car. As of October 2023, the following are the normal expenses for Rhine passenger ferries:

• Short Routes (e.g., Bingen to Rüdesheim): Around €5 • €10 per person, one way.

• Medium Routes (e.g., Königswinter to Bad Honnef): Foot travellers pay between €2 and €6.

• Longer routes (e.g., Mainz to Koblenz): Round-trip costs may vary from €15 to €25 per person.

• Car Transport: For individuals travelling by car, charges may increase dramatically, ranging between €20 and €40 depending on vehicle size and route.

Helpful Tips

Timetables: It is recommended that you check ferry timetables ahead of time, particularly during off-peak seasons, since they are subject to change.

Multi-trip Passes: Some ferry operators provide multi-trip passes or return discounts, which may help you save money on regularly travelled routes.

Scenic Cruises: Consider taking a scenic boat down the Rhine, which often includes meals and guided excursions, giving you a thorough view of the region.

Season: The summer months are the busiest, but travelling in the shoulder seasons (spring and autumn) may give a more relaxing experience with fewer people.

Currency and Payment Tips

The Rhine River, which flows through numerous nations in central Europe, provides a vital cultural and economic link. It crosses sections of Switzerland, Germany, France, Luxembourg, and the Netherlands. When travelling along the Rhine, whether for business or pleasure, it is essential to understand the currency and payment procedures of the areas you will be visiting. Here are some suggestions for managing cash and payments when travelling along the Rhine.

Currency

Euro (€):

• The Euro is the official currency of Germany, France, Luxembourg, and the Netherlands. Switzerland uses the Swiss Franc (CHF).

• Bring a combination of cash and cards, particularly when visiting smaller towns or rural regions where card acceptance may be restricted.

Currency Exchange:

- Currency exchange facilities are readily accessible in major cities, airports, and rail stations. However, they may demand a larger price than using ATMs.

- If you have Swiss Francs, be aware that not all Eurozone institutions will take them, and vice versa.

Payment Methods:

Credit and debit cards:

- Most places along the Rhine accept credit and debit cards, particularly in metropolitan areas. Visa and Mastercard are the most often accepted, however, American Express may be less so.

- Before travelling, call your bank to advise them of your intentions and prevent any problems with international transactions.

Contactless Payment:

- Contactless payments (NFC) are accepted by a large number of retailers, restaurants, and transportation providers. A mobile payment option, such as Apple Pay or Google Pay, might increase convenience.

Cash:

- While card payments are ubiquitous, keeping extra cash on hand is a good idea, particularly for little purchases, market booths, and areas where card payments are not accepted.

Withdrawal Tips

ATMs:

- ATMs are readily accessible and often provide competitive exchange rates. To save expenses, look for ATMs that are associated with your bank.

- Be aware of dynamic currency conversion (DCC) choices at ATMs and points of sale, since they might result in increased costs. It's typically preferable to pay in local money.

Withdrawal limits:

- Be mindful of the ATM withdrawal restrictions. It may be good to withdraw greater sums less often to save on costs.

Additional Tips:

Small Change:

- Keep tiny changes for public transit and small sellers. Many locations may not provide change for higher amounts.

Gratuities:

- Tipping methods differ. In restaurants, it is typical to round up the bill or leave a 5-10% tip. In bars, it is customary to round off your bill or leave tiny changes.

Travel Insurance:

- Consider purchasing travel insurance, which covers the loss or theft of money and possessions, offering peace of mind while travelling.

Budgeting:

- Base your budget on the areas you'll visit. Living expenses might vary greatly among nations. For example, Switzerland is far more costly than its neighbouring nations.

Health, Safety, and Insurance

Health considerations

Vaccinations: Before travelling, consult your healthcare practitioner about any required vaccinations. Tetanus, diphtheria, and maybe others are among the most common immunisations, depending on your health history and vaccination regimen.

Travel Insurance: It is advisable to have travel insurance that covers medical emergencies. This may shield you from hefty healthcare expenditures in the event of sickness or accident. Make sure the insurance covers abroad health care and provides 24-hour help.

Medication: If you use prescription prescriptions, make sure you pack enough for the whole journey, plus a little extra in case of delays. Bring a copy of your prescriptions and store the drugs in their original containers.

First Aid Kit: Bring a small first aid kit with necessities like adhesive bandages, antiseptic wipes, painkillers, allergy medications, and any other personal medical supplies you may need.

Hydration and Food Safety: Stay hydrated, particularly during outdoor activity. To reduce the risk of foodborne disease, dine at reputed restaurants. Be careful while eating street food, and make sure it's well-cooked.

Safety considerations

Personal Safety: The Rhine River area is typically safe for travellers. However, like with any trip location, be alert to your surroundings, particularly in busy areas. Keep your possessions secure and utilise hotel safes to store valuables.

Transportation: When travelling along the Rhine, choose trusted transportation services. This might involve railroads, buses, or organised river trips. If you are renting a vehicle, make sure you are acquainted with the local driving regulations and restrictions.

Outdoor Activities: If you want to participate in outdoor activities such as hiking or cycling, use suitable clothing and stick to defined pathways. Keep emergency contact information and local emergency numbers ready.

Weather Conditions: The Rhine Valley may encounter a variety of weather. Keep an eye on the weather and dress in layers. Prepare for rain or cold with waterproof coats and appropriate footwear.

COVID-19 recommendations: Keep current with any pandemic-related health recommendations. Understand the testing, immunisation, and masking requirements in your own country as well as the locations you want to travel to.

Insurance Considerations

Type of Insurance: Look for comprehensive travel insurance that covers medical emergencies, trip cancellations, lost baggage, and personal liability. Examine the policy's limitations and exclusions to guarantee proper coverage.

Emergency Coverage: Make sure your insurance covers emergency evacuation, particularly if you intend to go to more remote places. This is essential if you need to access medical facilities fast.

Activity Coverage: If you want to indulge in adventurous activities (such as bicycling, trekking, or river-based trips), be sure your insurance policy covers these activities.

Documentation: Keep both a digital and physical copy of your insurance policy and emergency contact information. Familiarise yourself with the process of submitting claims while overseas.

Local Health Services: Look for local hospitals and clinics along the Rhine River's path. Know how to reach them in case of an emergency.

Chapter 10 concludes with "Embrace the Magic of the Rhine."

Make the Most of Your River Journey

The Rhine River, one of Europe's most famous rivers, flows through gorgeous countryside, ancient towns, and bustling metropolis. A trip along the Rhine provides travellers with a unique combination of culture, natural beauty, and adventure. Whether you're floating on a fancy riverboat or visiting picturesque towns, here are some pointers to help you make the most of your Rhine River adventure.

Choose the right time to visit.

The Rhine River may be enjoyed all year, although the finest months for a river trip are often late spring to early fall. This time is distinguished by moderate weather and bright landscapes, including blossoming flowers and lush green vineyards. The fall months may also be memorable, especially for wine enthusiasts, since you can observe the grape harvest.

Plan your itinerary wisely.

The Rhine is bordered by extraordinary cities and towns, including:

• Basel: Known for its bustling cultural scene, museums, and breathtaking architecture.

• Strasbourg: A fusion of French and German traditions, with picturesque canals and the breathtaking Strasbourg Cathedral.

• Cologne: Known for its majestic cathedral and vibrant Old Town with beer gardens and shops.

• Rüdesheim: A lovely wine town famous for its Riesling wines and the quaint Drosselgasse street.

• Heidelberg: Home to Germany's oldest university and a breathtaking castle located on a hill.

When planning your trip, think about what interests you the most—whether it's history, gastronomy, or wine—and be sure to leave enough time to properly explore each place.

Immerse yourself with local culture.

Make your vacation unforgettable by participating in local customs and traditions. Local eateries provide regional foods such as sauerbraten, flammkuchen, and pretzels. Participating in a wine tasting or touring vineyards in the Rhine Valley might help you appreciate the region's viticulture.

If possible, go to local festivals or events. Markets, parades, and wine festivals are common throughout the summer months, providing opportunities to socialise with both residents and other travellers.

Explore Off the Beaten Path.

While large cities are worth visiting, tiny villages and hidden beauties along the Rhine should not be overlooked. Bacharach and Boppard have fairy-tale appeal and peaceful settings. Wander through the cobblestone streets, browse the small stores, and relax by the river.

Take advantage of scenic cruising.

One of the delights of the Rhine River voyage is the chance to sail through breathtaking scenery. The Rhine Gorge, which connects Koblenz and Bingen, is exceptionally attractive, with castles perched atop steep slopes and terraced vineyards cascading down to the water's edge. Make sure to bring your camera and take in the sights.

Use Guided Tours and Local Guides.

Consider including guided excursions in your schedule. Knowledgeable local guides may give insights into history, art, and culture that you may otherwise overlook. A guide may greatly improve your experience, whether you're browsing through museums, touring historical places, or mastering the complexity of wine-making.

Embrace outdoor activities

Beyond cultural discovery, the Rhine provides several outdoor activities. Hiking routes go through breathtaking landscapes and vineyards, providing spectacular views of the river. Cycling along the riverbanks is another popular alternative that enables you to cover more land while enjoying fresh air and breathtaking views.

Stay flexible.

While preparation is important, some of the finest moments come from unexpected finds. Leave some time in your calendar for spontaneous activities, such as staying longer at a nice café, visiting an unexpected art museum, or taking a local culinary class.

Capture your memories.

Remember to capture your adventure, from spectacular valley vistas to colourful town streets. Whether you use photography, writing, or social media to preserve your experiences, you will be able to relive your Rhine adventures long after you return home.

Final thoughts and farewell.

As our adventure down the breathtaking Rhine River draws to an end, it's time to reflect on the remarkable experiences and memories we've made together. This gorgeous canal, passing through stunning landscapes filled with attractive towns, stately castles, and luscious vineyards, has provided us with a mesmerising background for adventure and fellowship.

The Rhine's enchantment captured our hearts from the minute we got onboard. Each place we visited, from the colourful streets of Cologne to the fairy-tale beauty of Rüdesheim, helped us better grasp the region's rich culture and history. We've tried beautiful local wines, eaten great meals filled with flavour, and marvelled at the gorgeous architecture that conveys tales from the past.

Our excursion was more than simply sights and flavours. The shared laughter, meaningful chats, and warmth of newfound friendships made this tour very memorable. Whether we were enjoying strolls through cobblestone alleyways, sailing by magnificent vineyards, or just admiring the stunning views from the balcony, every moment was filled with delight and discovery.

As we say our goodbyes, let us keep the spirit of the Rhine River with us as a reminder of the beauty of travel, the pleasure of adventure, and the friendships made when we step away from our daily lives. The tales we've told and the friendships we've created will be inscribed in our hearts.

Thank you to our other travellers and the personnel for making our vacation an unforgettable experience. May the memories we've made motivate us to pursue new experiences and treasure the connections we've formed along the way. Here's to the next voyage; may it be as rewarding and enjoyable as this one. Until we meet again, safe travels, and goodbye!

Useful resources and contact information for arranging a vacation to the Rhine River:

Tourism Information: 1. Visit Rhine Valley (Rheinland-Pfalz) • Website: [www.rheinland-pfalz-tourismus.com].(https://www.rheinland-pfalz-tourismus.com)

• Contact: info@rlp-tourismus.de or +49 6131 967 300.

2. Germany Travel (Deutsche Zentrale für Tourismus) • Website: www.germany.travel • Contact: info@germany.travel / +49 69 974 640.

3. Baden-Württemberg Tourism.

 • Website: [www.tourismus-bw.de].(https://www.tourismus-bw.de) Contact info@tourismus-bw.de or +49 721 920 1999.

4. Rhine Romantic Route.

 • Website address: www.romantischer-rhein.de

 • Contact us at info@romantischer-rhein.de.

1. Viking River Cruises • Website: [www.vikingrivercruises.com].(https://www.vikingrivercruises.com) • Call 1-800-304-9616.

2. Tauck River Cruise

 • Website address: [www.tauck.com].(https://www.tauck.com) • Call 1-800-468-2825.

3. Scenic Luxury Cruises & Tours • Website: [www.scenicusa.com].(https://www.scenicusa.com) • Call 1-855-313-9468.

4. KD Rhine Shipping.

• Website: [www.k-d.com].(https://www.k-d.com) • Contact info@k-d.com or +49 180 5 222 333.

Transportation: 1. Deutsche Bahn (Train Services) • Website: [www.bahn.com]. (https://www.bahn.com) • Call +49 180 6 996 633 (local charges apply).

2. Ferries on the Rhine Local tourist information centres may give contact information for various ferry services that operate along the Rhine.

Accommodations: 1. Booking.com

• Website address: www.booking.com

• Email: customer.service@booking.com.

2. Airbnb: Website: [www.airbnb.com].(https://www.airbnb.com) • Email: help@airbnb.com.

Local Attractions: 1. The Lorelei Association

• Website address: www.lorelei.com • Contact info@lorelei.com.

2. Rhine wine regions

• Website address: www.vinorhein.de

• Contact us at info@vinorhein.de.

For general travel information, see the TravelHealthPro (Travel Health Information) website at [www.travelhealthpro.org.uk].(https://travelhealthpro.org.uk)

Bonus Section(Expert Photography Tips & Travel Journal)

Bunus 1: Common and helpful words to communicate with people when travelling along the Rhine River. The phrases are largely in German, which is the most generally spoken language in the area.

Basic greetings.

• Hallo! (Hi!)

• Good morning!

• Guten Tag!" (Good afternoon!)

Guten Abend! (Good evening!)

- Tschüss! (Bye!)

Polite Expressions

- Bite. (Please.)

Thank you: Danke. or Vielen Dank!. (Thank you very much!)

- Entschuldigung, (Excuse me).

- I am sorry.

Asking for Assistance or Information

- Sprechen Sie Englisch? (Can you speak English?)

- Could you please help me? (Could you assist me?)

Wo ist...? (Where is...?)

- Das nächste Restaurant? (Where is the closest restaurant?)

Die Toilette? (The lavatory?)

- Der Bahnhof? (What about the rail station?)

Dining and Shopping: Ich hätte gerne...

- The bill, please. • Can I see the menu, please? (May I view the menu, please?)

- Wie viel kostet das? (What does this cost?)

Directions: Wie komme ich zu... (How do I get there?)

- Dem Fluss? (The river?)

- das Schloss? (the castle?)

Is it far from here?

Local Interaction.

- Was empfehlen Sie? (What would you suggest?)

- Könnte ich bitte ein Foto machen? (May I take a photograph, please?)

- What is usual for this area?

Weather and General Conversation

• Wie ist das Wetter heute? (What is the weather today?)

• It is gorgeous here.

• Have you always had a lot of visitors here?

Farewells

• Ich wünsche Ihnen einen schönen Tag!.

Auf Wiedersehen! (Goodbye!)

These words should assist you in negotiating discussions and interactions with locals when travelling along the Rhine.

Subject: We value your feedback! Help us improve your Rhine River experience

Bonus 2: Expert Photography Tips for Your Rhine Cruise

Capturing the stunning scenery of the Rhine River is an essential part of your journey. These expert tips will help you make the most of every shot, whether you're using a smartphone or a professional camera:

1. **Golden Hour Advantage**: Take photos during sunrise or sunset for soft, natural light that enhances landscapes and adds a warm glow to castles, vineyards, and riverbanks.

2. **Rule of Thirds**: Use the grid feature on your camera or phone to compose balanced shots by aligning key elements along the gridlines.

3. **Focus on Details**: Capture close-up shots of intricate castle carvings, vibrant flowers in villages, or the textures of cobblestone streets.

4. **Reflections on Water**: Look for reflections of castles or trees on the river for a serene, mirror-like effect. Use a tripod for a steady shot.

5. **Framing with Nature**: Use tree branches, arches, or windows to frame your subject, adding depth and a natural border to your photos.

6. **Adjust for Motion**: If photographing from a moving boat, use a fast shutter speed or your phone's "action mode" to keep images sharp.

7. **Low-Light Shots**: For evening or indoor photos, increase ISO settings or use your phone's night mode to maintain clarity.

8. **Include People**: Add life to your shots by capturing friends, family, or locals against picturesque backdrops.

9. **Panoramic Views**: Use the panoramic feature to capture the sweeping landscapes of terraced vineyards and castle-studded horizons.

10. **Experiment with Angles**: Shoot from high viewpoints for vast landscapes or low angles to emphasize towering castles.

11. **Use Leading Lines**: Roads, rivers, or pathways guide the viewer's eye into the frame, creating visually compelling photos.

12. **HDR Mode**: Use High Dynamic Range mode to balance light and shadows, especially on bright sunny days.

13. **Cloudy Day Advantage**: Overcast skies reduce harsh shadows and bring out rich colors in your photos.

14. **Capture Candid Moments**: Document spontaneous moments like enjoying a meal, walking through villages, or chatting with locals for authentic memories.

15. **Edit Thoughtfully**: After your trip, use editing apps to enhance colors, crop unnecessary elements, or adjust brightness while keeping your photos natural.

With these tips, you'll return home with a gallery of stunning images that truly capture the essence of your Rhine adventure!

Bonus 3: Travel Journal in a tabular format for your Rhine Cruise adventure

Date	Destination/Stop	Key Activities/Excursions	Memorable Moments	Food Tried/Restaurants	Thoughts & Reflections	Photos Taken (Yes/No)
Day 1						
Day 2						
Day 3						
Day 4						
Day 5						
Day 6						
Day 7						
Packing List:		Special Memories to Remember:			Important Contacts/Information	

This journal allows space to record everything from day-to-day experiences to personal reflections, helping you cherish every moment of your trip.

Dear readers,

Dear Reader,

Thank you for choosing this guide to accompany you on your Rhine River Cruise journey. It means the world to me that you've entrusted my work to help make your experience unforgettable.

As a travel guide writer, every word in this book represents hours of research, countless resources, and personal experiences gathered during my own visits to the Rhine. Exploring the historic castles, charming villages, and breathtaking landscapes of this magnificent river took time, effort, and dedication, all with one goal in mind—to provide you with the most practical and enjoyable guide possible.

Your thoughts, feedback, and positive reviews are more than just words to me—they are a testament to the work I've poured my heart into. They help me improve, inspire others to explore the wonders of the Rhine, and motivate me to continue creating guides that make travel easier and more meaningful for others.

If you've found this book useful or feel it added value to your trip, I kindly ask you to leave a review. Your feedback not only supports my progress as a writer but also allows me to continue sharing the magic of travel with others like you.

Thank you for being a part of this journey with me, and I wish you unforgettable moments on your Rhine River Cruise!

Warm regards.

Darrin C. Ervin

Made in the USA
Columbia, SC
13 February 2025